IT REVOLUTION IN ARCHITETTURA

series edited by Antonino Saggio

1

EDILSTAMPA
editrice dell'ANCE

COVER
Blur Building, Lake Neuchatel, Yverdon-les-Bains, Switzerland, 2002

PHOTO CREDITS
Glenn Halvorson, p. 24-25
Michael Moran, p. 36-37, 56-57, 60, 77
Tina Barney, p. 45
John Louie, p. 48
Beat Widmer, p. 80-81, 84-85.

The projects Facsimile (p. 48), Institute of Contemporary Art (p. 65), Eyebeam Museum of Art & Technology (p. 68-69, 72-73), Lincoln Center for the Performing Arts (p. 76), Slither Building (p. 77) were created with Charles Renfro and signed Diller Scofidio + Renfro

TRANSLATION FROM ITALIAN
Christine Tilley

LAYOUT
Pasquale Strazza

Edilstampa srl
Via Guattani, 24
00161 Roma
tel. 0684567403
fax 0644232981
www.edilstampa.ance.it

FIRST EDITION IN ITALIAN
Rome, October 2005

ENGLISH EDITION
Rome, september 2011

Antonello Marotta

Diller + Scofidio
Blurred Theater

preface by Antonino Saggio

To Felice and Anna

Special thanks to Christine Tilley for amicably devoting her time to the translation of the text into English, to Barbara Pasqualetto for support in the translation of research material and to Denise Fasanello for her assistance in the two years of contacts between the author and Diller&Scofidio's offices. Special thanks to Elizabeth Diller and Ricardo Scofidio who have devoted their attention to this editorial project and provided the graphic material, and for the detailed interview included in this book. My deep gratitude to Antonino Saggio for his fundamental guidance.

The numbers beside the text refer to the pages showing illustrations of the projects mentioned.

The mental landscape

preface by Antonino Saggio

In the minds of the new generation of architects, who we once said were "born with the computer", a new landscape has been taking shape for years, a landscape generated by the new era: the landscape of information.
What are its fundamental components? First of all, within this world, information takes on great value, it is the true raw material. It fluctuates, reconfigures, shapes itself into significant, productive forms, then shifts to coagulate again in a different way. A great distance from the past is felt, understood, sensed in this mental landscape. If cogwheels, piston rods and conveyor belts were the bricks and mortar (and sources of inspiration) of a mechanical, industrial landscape, to be built up by Gropius, Mies, Le Corbusier and Wright, nowadays, and even more tomorrow, it is information "bits" that represent the indispensable denomination of a contemporary world jostling to take shape in architecture, too. A second element of this new mental landscape is its similarity with what we experience more and more each day. Today's landscape is not just the contemporary metropolis in its changing shape in various corners of the world, but also, and above all, what we experience each minute on our computer screens and in our technological "limbs". A landscape made up of leaps, overlays, above all of dynamic interconnections between information. It is the landscape of interactivity.
Then, finally, there is at least a third element to the mental landscape indistinctly taking shape in the minds of the new artists and architects. That of nature regained, nature once more actively participating in the contemporary world and no longer relegated to display tray for the shiny objects of machinery. This retrieved nature weaves through the research on complexity permitted by electronic models, and breathes through the mutations and hybridization of our body, appearing as an active, intelligent sister beside architecture.
For years the blending of these three elements of the new mental landscape (information, interactivity, nature) in a work of architecture has been sought. A work that could condense their rationale and with its illustrative strength appear as the discovery

that would also make some new possibility feasible to others.
The great well-known strength of Elizabeth Diller & Ricardo Scofidio was to have created this work, to have blended these elements in built architecture.
As many will know, we refer to the *Blur Building* at Yverdon-les-Bains, created for the Swiss Expo of 2002. The building breaks with all previous conventions in architecture and sets itself up as an authentic new paradigm for the architecture of the future.
Here at Yverdon-les-Bains the building (clearly made of flesh and blood, in this case a metallic framework) never stays the same. The great oval structure on stilts 90 meters long "is" in this case, first and foremost, information. By a complex system of sensors the building constantly changes as certain parameters for reading the external information change. The degree of humidity, temperature and wind are all measured by a series of sensors that via transformation programs control thousands of nozzles spraying nebulised water in various ways. The mist constantly changes with respect to the building, continuously altering it, sometimes making a prow emerge, then a terrace, or a bridge, or nothing. Without the reading and transformation of the environmental information, there would simply be the pure metallic skeleton of a panoramic platform (beautiful in itself, nonetheless, à la Buckminster Fuller). The *Blur* story is not, however, an extreme view of industrialization but was wholly projected into the 21st century, part of the past history still to be written of the computerization of architecture.
One might ask how the building manages to move in the world of dynamic interconnections and interactivity so present in our everyday digital existence? Here the idea itself of a building as a static, closed, autonomous and basically non-reactive entity has been eliminated. The building is an element of transformation, it changes as conditions change, and as the program deciding which input to use (in this case meteorological variations) and which output to generate (in this case the intensity of the sprays) changes. But, as is obvious, and as other buildings at the same Expo 2002 demonstrated, we can alter both input and output and in some cases even leave one or the other somewhat indefinite. In this scenario the building acts as an element of transformation, as the mediator between situations, desires and conditions.
Finally, perhaps we should mention the new presence of nature?

For those who have had the fortune to see the *Blur Building* transformed at night, revealing then hiding itself, changing the lake-water into mist, turning lights into stars, no doubts remain on the new alliance displayed here between architecture and nature.
In this context, the book you are holding, written by Antonello Marotta, already the author of a valued text on Ben van Berkel and many other essays and articles, carries out a fundamental role. The author explains to us how the innovative intensity of the *Blur* is born from a strong, original, innovative research trend, very different from the traditional ones.
Diller and Scofidio have worked in an intermediate sphere for over two decades, moving between art installations, philosophy, displays, performances and, of course, teaching, in particular at the New York Cooper Union. This pathway has led the two architects to experiment in first person with contemporary thought, sowing the seeds of various elements of the new mental landscape while they worked with artists, performers, dancers, stage designers.
With his enthusiastic work Marotta gives us one of the most complete, detailed texts on Diller and Scofidio: an accurate, analytical book, permeated by persuasive images both in his writing and in the iconographic accompaniment enriched with original quotations that emerged from Elizabeth Diller's keen participation in the writing of the book and the choice of iconographic material. The outcome for the reader, who might like to follow up the useful bibliographical references, will be indicative of new paths to explore.

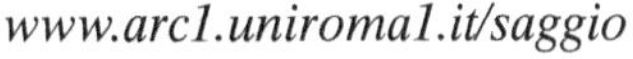
www.arc1.uniroma1.it/saggio

1. The 70s, the Apple rebels

1.1 Outside the system

The international culture of the 60s and 70s was marked by an invisible line that linked New York to Europe. The flight from Nazi Germany had catapulted the greatest masters of European rationalism across to America, creating fertile land for the birth of a design philosophy which would decide the fortune of many American studios. If, on the one hand, the London Architectural Association was the school that catalyzed the most important European practice, with Bernard Tschumi, Daniel Libeskind, Rem Koolhaas and Elia Zenghelis among those who taught there, New York was certainly the other axis on which a variety of artistic and architectural experiments saw the seeds of a complex, unexpected history flower. In the great Apple the university that was the driving force was Cooper Union. John Hejduk delimited the School's guidelines with his syllabus. Studies on the grid, the square and the value of number were aimed at determining transferable knowledge, but at the same time Hejduk did not lose sight of the abstract value of architecture and was able to generate a revival of Le Corbusier's spirit with new life-blood. Elizabeth Diller trained at Cooper Union, when Ricardo Scofidio was already teaching there halfway through the 60s. Before beginning his collaboration with Diller, Scofidio already had a vast background and ran an important studio. Diller's artistic course is extremely interesting. She studied photography and film before transferring to the architecture courses. Revisited today, drafts of the work she developed in those years bear witness to her highly intuitive worth, from her labyrinthine drawings to a chair designed in 1978, made of rope, fabric, wood and rubber, a warning of a sense of weakness and nomadism.

One year after my graduation from Cooper Union (Diller), I proudly showed John Hejduk my first, fledgling, self-directed project. Instead of giving me the approval I so eagerly expected and craved, Hejduk remarked, "I cleared the jungle so that you could ride your tricycle?" I was crushed but soon grew to understand that independent work in architecture was not going to be championed by anyone, it had to aggravate everyone. I also began to understand that his role in producing a climate of tolerance for independent work came with much struggle. But that climate of tolerance in the 70s became increasingly intolerant to external influences in the 80s and 90s. As the school stayed clear of the "corrupting" profession, it sealed itself off from everything but canonical Modernism and high culture. This new orthodoxy was suffocating and led me to gravitate to the excluded: the Venturis, Smithson, Matta-Clark, performance art, and fashion. And myself (Scofidio) to jazz, automobile design, and pulp fiction (D + S 2004).

In 1979 Ricardo Scofidio and Elizabeth Diller created an interdisciplinary studio in New York which pursued a particular line of confluence between various arts including architecture, the new media, the spectacle and the performance. In the 80s, while research in Europe was intent on defining architecture in relation to place identity, place being profoundly urban and relating to mankind – to the point that the *genius loci* investigated by Christian Norberg-Schulz almost became a slogan for it – Diller and Scofidio began a critical review of the approach to architecture. This aimed at a new definition of site, meant, in their interpretation, as a physical space addressing the ritual and political identity involving man in the social context.

D+S emerged in the 1980s at a time when architect/academics like Eisenman, Tschumi and Libeskind used print and the gallery as their forum. That approach was too detached for us. We were determined to materialize our work in full scale and in public space. As the "Paper Architects" of the 80s evolved professional building practices in the 90s, we resisted the temptation of financial stability to maintain our uncompromised critical stance. Much of our early work was self-generated and built on borrowed or stolen sites and funded by grants or loans. Often, we collaborated with artists, experimental theater groups, and not-for-profit organizations. Our position "outside the system" yet within the public realm led us to alternative modes such as architectural installations and multi-media theater hybrids. The guerrilla tactics of the early work led to no-strings-attached projects commissioned by established cultural institutions like MoMA and the Walker, which led to our
first architectural commissions such as the *Slow House* for a Japanese art **32-33**
collector and the *Gifu Housing* project with Arata Isozaki as the **77**
masterplanner. These first architectural commissions came from an appreciation of our independent work (D + S 2004).

Intuitive, enigmatic and unconventional, D + S evaded the official culture for decades. If they were asked whether they considered themselves artists or architects, they usually answered: "We tell the architects we're artists and the artists that we're architects".
In a noteworthy essay on the American duo emblematically

entitled *Erasure and disembodiment*, Georges Teyssot traced an initial profile of them: "They have specialised in the following fields: body-building, squash, motor-racing, baseball, hygiene, androgyny, the spreading of paranoia and disease of all kinds, American industrial design, demography, uniforms, etiquette, anatomic sketches, surgical appliances and probes. They like to eat in a messy way, watch TV during the day, advertising, automobile culture, robotics, electronics, computer viruses, cartography and drawings made unconsciously from domestic objects" (Teyssot 90).
From these beginnings and in these fields D + S were to orient their efforts with an uncensored gaze, like an ethnographer studying primitive societies. They reconfigured architecture, intervening by using electronic transformation technologies. In their philosophy, architecture translates into a surgical instrument that operates on itself, highlighting everything that takes on new life.

1.2 The body without organs

In the years when academia was building solid walls to preserve its own foundations, Diller + Scofidio carried out important research, departing from the world of art and philosophy, to understand the social and political connections between the body, "meant as a surface susceptible to an excess of meanings" (D + S in Teyssot 90), and public space.

> Architecture is too preoccupied with formalism and disengaged from its socio-political context. Our first book, *Flesh*, established that architecture is not only about buildings; it is first and foremost about spatial relations. In fact, spatial relations precede architecture... beginning with the division of undifferentiated space into progressively smaller parcels and the setting up of legal and social distinctions between nations, neighbors, and even "his" and "hers". We argue that the human body is a cultural given and an irreducible site of regulation. *Flesh* begins with the legal definition of the buttocks outlined by Florida law - specifically how much flesh can legally cross the line into civic space to warrant the distinction of "indecent public exposure". Through the book, we trace the inextricable relation between bodies and the spatial conventions of the everyday (D + S 2004).

If the Modern Movement had realized New Objectivity (*Neue Sachlichkeit*) aesthetics, the dimension the architects investigated addressed New Subjectivity.
"In the awareness of the 20s and of New Objectivity a direct relationship was pursued between a space, and therefore a "spatial organ", and its function (with a meaning given to this term that could be associated with that of traditional medicine in which it is maintained that an organ is connected with a "particular" task). This is why the center was internal space, the idea of internal space as the engine of architecture. Well it was exactly this idea that in fact changed and was greatly enriched. In these last ten to fifteen years a spatial concept has strongly permeated it which has as its engine a concerted idea of internal-external, making public space just as fundamental an element of architecture" (Saggio 2000).
This new dimension generated a profound revolution: architecture exists before construction. The new guidelines concern the rejection of functionalism, attention to places of passing through and crossing and the loss of the delimitation of enclosure-space.
To understand the new scenarios of the shift from "organic" to "inorganic" we need to retrieve Deleuze and Guattari's *Anti-Oedipus*, written in 1972, in which the theory of the body without organs is set out; they suggest the mechanistic, regulated view of the human body is outdated, and develop the concept of desire as a historic and social force. The philosophers unleashed the idea that desire is moved by a lack or need, which derived from psychoanalytical theories and Marxism, and understood it as production and flow, a process of concatenations. D + S adopted this view: "Deleuze explains: the body without organs is not opposed to organs, as such, but to the organism; as the body is identified with hierarchies and organized by an internal logic of functioning, it lacks the variety of directives that are kindled by desire" (D + S in Teyssot 90).
This means considering the many levels of "subjectivity of desires" compared with the "objectivity of needs" with which the Modern Movement had established the rules of inhabiting.
D + S developed this observation point from the artistic movements springing up in the New York of the 60s and 70s, which were staging the new subject in social space. Acconci's *body performances* and *guerilla art* were to mark a point of no return in them, generating research from then onwards that was totally

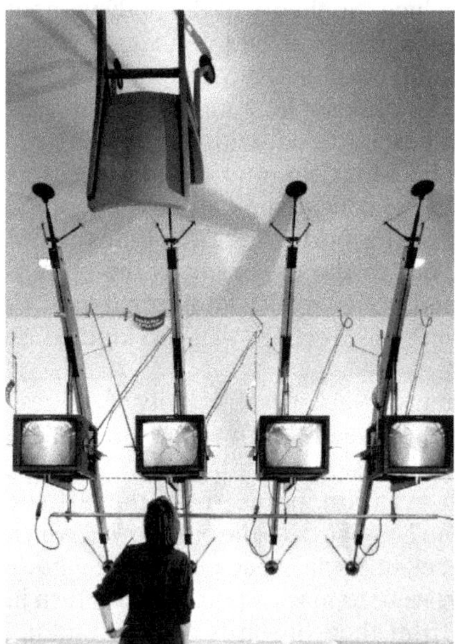

PARA-SITE, *THE MUSEUM OF MODERN ART, NEW YORK, 1989*

In this installation they take up the themes the French philosopher Michel Serres developed in The parasite *(1982). The relationship between host body (museum) and parasite (installation) constitutes the cornerstone of this performance.*

On the opposite page:
THE WITHDRAWING ROOM, *CAPP STREET PROJECT, SAN FRANCISCO, 1987*

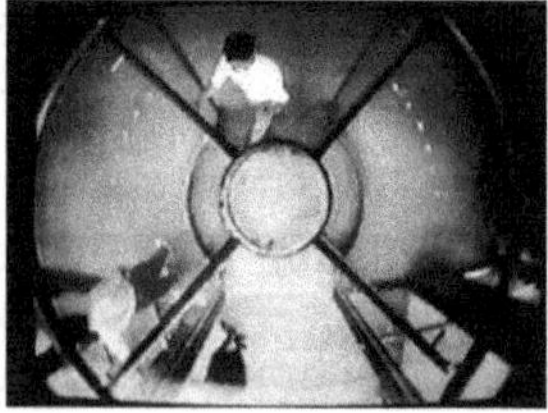

intent on the new definition of space.

> As much as Hejduk was the guru, the most profound influence during the Cooper years for me (Diller) was an older classmate that was also a musician with Steve Reich and Phil Glass. He introduced me to the work of those composers as well as choreographers like Trisha Brown and theater artists such as Richard Foreman and the Wooster Group. The work of Acconci and Laurie Anderson was particularly compelling as it fused the discrete categories of art, performance, and political activity. That was the difference. Artistic endeavour at that time used a variety of media strategies to speak about cultural and political issues. Architecture was helplessly inarticulate in speaking about anything but itself (D + S 2004).

The Happenings of the 60s had brought artistic expression back to a more audio and visual concept of theater, a theater that had everyday life as its field of processes and relations and considered the body stripped of social conventions. Translation of the ordinary became the new tragic field, where subject and object of the scene portrayed themselves and channelled the energy of the artist-work into the body projected towards change. In Performance Art the body became the new medium, to express information concerning the psyche and re-establish contact with the senses. Rauschenberg's performances with Cunningham and Cage, Trisha Brown, Laurie Anderson and Vito Acconci combined dance, gymnastics, music, sound and video. The ritual tended to involve the spectator directly and bridge the passive gap that had characterized past practice. The use of the new media (television, photography, film) brought social, gestural and procedural technology onto the scene, which was inexorably transforming the observer's sensory perception.

The society that D + S were investigating and narrating was largely shaped by the new media. Their survey addressed a field of observation that involved man in relation to the technologies that were exploring him, marking, scrutinizing and regulating him.

2. New rites

2.1 Prosthetic Theory

D + S quickly explored and developed a series of pathways: the culture of gender, the issue of security and control, domesticity, which delved into everyday life to reveal its hidden codes and the culture of the spectacle, ensuing from their directly witnessing the season of Pop Art, where consumer objects became the new objects of collective desire, as cleverly expressed in Warhol's works.

In the *site-specific* installations they developed a field of forces in which the space where they were positioned was built from the standpoint of the observer, and of a new awareness that interaction develops. It is not easy to penetrate the D + S universe if not through their gaze – disenchanted and searching, ironic and paradoxical – which analyses society with a critical conscience, often shocking. Society was changing its behavioral rituals urged on by the new media and electronic technologies. In both their theoretical and project work they analyse the shift from the society of machines to that of information, via the mass media culture that determined this transition. The society of machines had been portrayed in a masterly, bizarre way in the film *Modern Times* (1936), in which Chaplin played the part of a factory-worker who, subjected to the exhausting pace of the assembly-line and watched by closed-circuit TV, took on the frantic behavior of production machinery. In the same period, in Le Corbusier's theories architecture was likened to a machine to be lived in. Modernism had basically catalyzed this energy in favour of the production system. In the 50s American Study House propaganda images shifted their attention to the technological tools that "freed" women, at least in the words of the advertisements, from slaving over housework.

Between the society of machines and the new territories of electronics and the virtual, a tendency had begun to open up in the 70s which incorporated design, film, science fiction and the new scientific discoveries addressing artificial intelligence construction: androids and cyborgs. The theme of prosthetics, mechanical and electronic limbs, of technology as a tool of reinforcement, found its grounds in time in the need to extend the

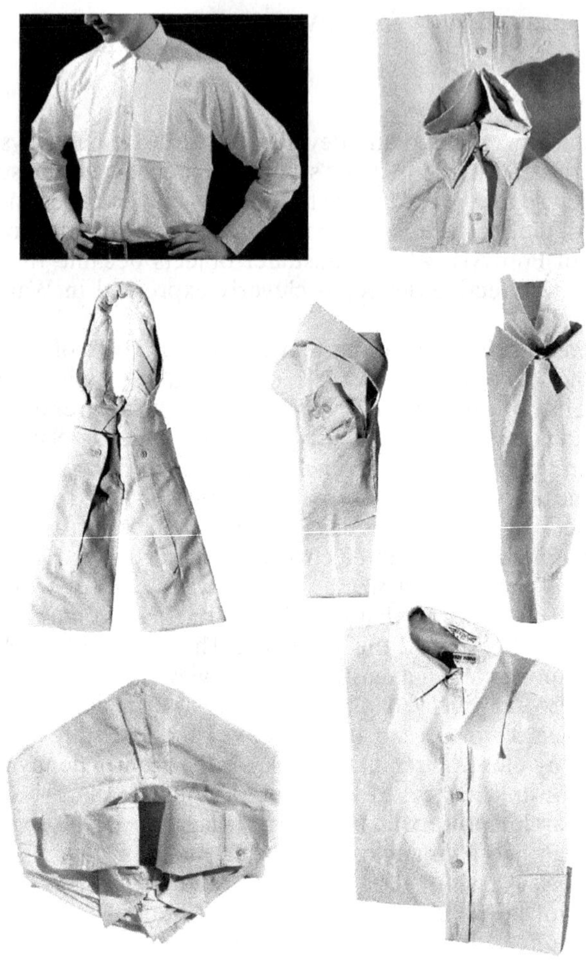

BAD PRESS: DISSIDENT HOUSEWORK SERIES, *1993-1998*

Departing from the identity of the post-industrial body expressed by Deleuze, D + S interpret the fold as a multiple, mutant surface. In this installation they challenge the world of categories and standards through dissident ironing.

On the opposite page:
THE ROTARY NOTARY AND HIS HOT PLATE (DELAY IN GLASS), *THE PAINTED BRIDE ART CENTER, PHILADELPHIA, 1987*

physical energy of the body, generating hybrids between man and machine, nature and artifice.

D + S broke up the linguistic and lexical structure of the conventional academic body of architecture; their gaze focused intently on cinema and theater. Towards the end of the 70s cinematography began to predict a dimension in which the body – having superseded the fantastic explorations inside it of the 60s using a scale-jump down to miniature men – moved towards the insertion of foreign bodies into the abdomen, like in the field of medicine, from video cassettes to aliens: suffice it to think of the themes dealt with by David Cronenberg in Videodrome (1983) or Ridley Scott's Alien (1979). In this view the body, subjected to the incorporation of parasites within it, becomes vulnerable.

12 *Para-site* is the title of an installation D + S realised in 1989 in the Projects Room of New York's Museum of Modern Art. They took up again the themes that the French philosopher Michel Serres had developed in *The parasite* (1982). The cornerstone of this performance was the institutionalized place of the museum hosting the exhibition. By nature the parasite lives in a specific place and in a relationship with the body hosting it. D + S interpreted the theme of vision, in its various versions, where the visitor observes and is at the same time subjected to surveillance. The parasite is the installation itself which violates the institutionalized place of the museum. This all leads back to a prosthetic dimension, of machine-monitor yielding images re-oriented by 90° or 180°, which show the control and safety systems of the museum. As in Jeremy Bentham's *Panopticon* structure, however, the institution observes the visitor who cannot observe himself in real time on the monitor. In this dimension public and private are hybridized in an ambiguous space which, basically, modifies them both. D + S highlight their being artists, intellectuals, in a dimension with widespread limits. But their spaces enjoy details, maintaining etymologically the "cutting" interpretation, great control and elegance. Design is realized like a prosthesis, an alien environment, with chairs anchored to the ceiling, on which quotations are printed of texts by Serres and Bentham, which can be stamped onto the flesh of a hypothetical occupier. The chairs celebrate everything but comfort and bring
13 back to mind the 1987 installation The *withDrawing Room*, where the theme of propriety is handled. The architects inquire into the

theme of domesticity, explored through the aesthetics of assembling and mounting objects of everyday use: a table, chairs, a bed. These elements, which in Modernism constituted the raw material to strengthen the idea of an objective space, in D + S's critical review enter inexorably into conflict with the space of inhabiting, to the point of losing unity in prosthetic objects, sectioned or placed on unusable planes. Space generates a sort of dislocation in which the contrast between internal/external, public/private, form/function loses its meaning.

To go back to the *Para-site* installation, monitors in the galleries show images of TV cameras placed in three locations: the principal entrance, where those entering are subjected to surveillance, the escalator space, giving partial images of the bodies that ascend and descend, and the external space of the garden of sculptures. D + S intended to fragment the view of the public and make perception complex, where the real and the fake are mixed and hybridized.

Architecture has reconfigured its own substance incorporating electronic technology.

When Mark Wigley published the article *Prosthetic Theory: The Disciplining of Architecture* in Assemblage in 1991 he clarified that: "Digital prosthetic architecture is what remains of what was the solid body of the university. The critical gap between architecture and its metaphor has been abolished. The ancient dwelling of the theorist and theory is electronic [...] The way these parasite technologies inhabit, infect and enter into symbiosis with the body of architecture redefines the issue" (Wigley 90).

D + S anticipated by a few years an architecture that, as Wigley asserted, was altered by its technological offspring, inviting us to enter into the new virtual code.

2.2 The bachelor machine

The American duo devoted an important part of their research to redefining and challenging gender conventions, based on the social organization of sexual differences. Their critical gaze turned habits and the slots into which roles and behaviors were assigned upside down. The stereotype view of women triggered their arguments.

Diller and Scofidio were dazzled by Duchamp's intuitions, the

artist who in the 20s acknowledged the culture of dissociated groups like the *Hydropathes* in France or the *Scapigliatura* in Italy, taking up the rejection and denial of the *bourgeois* society and the positivist idea of progress. The art of negation, the crisis of the concept of standardized function, the *nihil* as artistic expression. His greatest contribution would go to architects like Peter Eisenman and Zaha Hadid who, recuperating the sense of movement from Duchamp's stroboscopic works, generated fluid and dynamic spaces via digital techniques.
Through conceptual processes Duchamp had shifted the attention away from objects to the relations between objects, opening the way to art that caused surprise, staged the absurd, when almost at the same time Picasso was creating *Les Demoiselles d'Avignon* (1907) aiming at a complex construction of the human shape in space.
Why Duchamp and what role did he play?

> Duchamp was the first to challenge the institution of art, the authority of the gallery, notions of authenticity, and the boundaries between media. These continue to be critical themes for artists working in every discipline today. But the most important aspects of Duchamp's work for us were the interweaving of visual and textual forms of expression (D + S 2004).

Between 1915 and 1923 Duchamp created *La mariée mise à nu par ses célibataires (The bride stripped bare by her bachelors, even)*, better known as *Le Grand Verre (The Large Glass)*, a large plate of glass three meters high, the brilliant artist's masterpiece.
André Breton considered that in this work *human love was seen by a being from another planet.* As destiny would have it, the glass broke during a journey, causing some series of fractures that Duchamp saw as the proper, thorough completion of his work.
In 1987 Diller and Scofidio took inspiration from the work
quoted, creating the performance *The rotary notary and his hot*
17 *plate (Delay in glass)*, written and produced by Susan Mosakowski
at the Painted Bride Art Center in Philadelphia, on the occasion of
the centenary of Duchamp's birth.
The underlying theme of the theatrical action is incommunicability. The bride and the bachelor, two separate, non-compliant entities, are given two different positions in the stage space. The stage is thus divided into two halves: one becomes the bride's field of action, the other that of the bachelor. A constructed device that

highlights this mixture of theater and architecture, it is based on a system that permits hiding and revealing. The plane can rotate 360°, showing in turn either the bride or the bachelor. The innovative aspect of the machine is a mirror suspended at 45° which shows the public the hidden person. The process thus tends to determine a shift of meaning from actual portrayal to a virtual level, in which the roles are confused. The mirror sloping at 45° reverses the physical places of the Cartesian axes, so that the floor is transformed into the reflected image on a vertical plane. The play of mirrors belongs to Renaissance culture, with Holbein's studies on anamorphosis, but reality, instead of being deformed, is duplicated, and the spectator can simultaneously experience and observe the real image of the bachelor and the reflected one of the bride. Dream and reality, fiction and the real do not portray two separate planes, but cohabit at different levels, tragically and absurdly true. Departing from the Dada artist's work, D + S recuperate the passage from the two-dimensional plane to a conceptual, visual, n-dimensional one, which channels onto the stage the fleeting dimension of the mirror and the virtual.
By this they intend to show the technology that bares the bride and makes visible the actual cultural process. D + S clarify the intention of their project: "In the Bachelor's bed, the head of the Bachelor penetrates the headboard towards the public; in this way the public sees the head directly, with his reflected body floating higher up. The Bachelor's disembodied head recites a chain of orders to his decapitated body. The bride lies on her back on the floor below. She is reflected floating as "the object of desire". The wall can rotate on a pivot to enable the characters to change position and also sexual identity" (D + S in Teyssot 90).
The instability of the stage construction highlights the increasingly less defined identity of man and woman, and social instability that becomes an act of reflection. At the end of the piece the virtual mirror D + S use in *Delay in Glass* slopes to depict the observing public itself, the heart and center of the story told, a place itself of reflection, in agreement with Duchamp's thought which considered that in the *Large Glass* the observer could reflect his/her most intimate nature.

2.3 Travel and new territories

Particular attention was paid by D + S to the conventional processes linked with tourist travel that ventured towards politically unstable territories. In 1991 they created the installation
24-25 *Tourism: suitCase Studies*, where they staged some of the themes they investigated.

> Mildred Friedman, the curator of the Walker Art Center asked us to make a site-specific installation about a theme in contemporary architecture. The show would travel to four other museums around the country. The paradox of a traveling site-specific installation became the object of our fascination. Travel and tourism would become the theme, particularly travel to the national past (D + S 2004).

The official culture had always endeavored to seek uncontaminated places, with artists, writers and poets traveling towards virgin territories from where they could study the hidden sense of immediate things. A thin borderline urged national identities to seek in other places a dimension of authenticity by now considered lost. Such travels have characterized all historic periods, but a great attraction for them was certainly felt in the 1900s. Nowadays the speed of travel compared with the slow journeys by carriage has caused a loss of territorial values in favor of an assortment of information strongly characterizing our times. Geography translates into a mutant system: a discipline undergoing metamorphosis, as Foucault has theorized. The values of *acceleration, map* and *extreme* have substituted the principles of authenticity.

In American tourism culture, the authentic past is re-proposed as theater fiction which combines myth, rituality and historic events, dressed and wrapped to appeal to popular fantasy. Time, historic space and geography itself are negotiable. The construction of imitation realities (Lincoln's fake house, the fake Alamo, the fake Athens Acropolis) does not seem to cause the tourist any problem. The ritualized past is rid of a series of not very noble situations. History is altered to appeal to the public. Architects place the emphasis on the voyeur aspect of the conventional tourist. In the end it is indeed the tourist who wants to depict history according to his/her critical and aesthetic canons; the market does nothing more than support these desires. History is rewritten in a sort of pact stipulated between the tourist and the market behind it.

The serial installation in 50 Samsonite suitcases, one from each of the 50 states in the US, concentrated on two types of sites in which heroism and authenticity played a large role: famous beds and famous battlefields (D + S 2004).

D + S play with conventional desires and in the collective imagination the bed represents the most private, personal space, the place where the breath of the historic figure can be perceived. If this designates private space, then public space is marked by the battle-field on which we can revisit heroes' deeds in our imagination. Images of maps, drawings, models, philosophy texts and postcards flutter in displays. The architects challenge the codes of sight, unmasking the myth of authenticity and with it mocking at the postcards and souvenirs, faded testimonies of the history of the place. The suitcases were arranged in the alphabetical order of the American states, placed in 5 rows of 10 and numbered according to the economic order each state obtained in the tourist market. In this work on the theme of travel D + S introduced a dimension in itself a tourist one, via a journey of the mind. Mobility was an integral part of the installation, kept in mind for the journey to the following exhibition place. A sort of display-case was thus created. Screens that were rotated at 45° and anchored to the ceiling with a telescopic axis, led the visitor's mind into a profoundly conceptual environment. Their work was pervaded by a connecting logic of assembled elements that yielded the complexity of the montage and the message. At the end of the installation the suitcases were closed, enclosing all the parts – structural, technological, conceptual – that composed them and with them all the sensations they were able to generate. D + S realize system-works, their parts connected and assembled to generate emotions and memories, to disclose what we accept passively, until we become aware of it.

2.4 The sensitive fold

Compared with the Modernist theories which considered the body of architecture subjected to rules for mechanical functioning and minimal consumption, D + S soon began to challenge those

TOURISMS: SUITCASE STUDIES,
WALKER ART CENTER, MINNEAPOLIS, 1991

The installation of 50 Samsonite suitcases analyzed two types of site: famous beds and important battlefields, where authenticity and heroism played a central role. The suitcases were arranged in the alphabetical order of the American states, placed in 5 rows of 10 and numbered according to the economic order each state obtained in the tourist market. The installation was realized as a sort of screen on which the myth of authenticity was challenged.

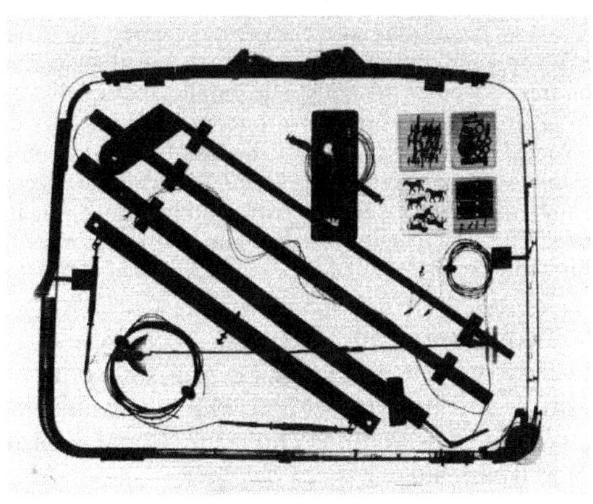

traditional systems that had generated the worlds of categories and standards, both cultural and behavioral, eliminating the idea that architecture had necessarily to express values of comfort and functionality. The American duo concentrated on the rituals of domesticity, from obsession with health to the pathologies of hygiene, which though hidden and disguised represent the heart of domestic space. They put life on the stage, showing its contradictions.

In 1993 Liz Diller and Ricardo Scofidio created the installation
16 *Bad Press* which would be exhibited in 1998 at the Venice Biennial 6th International Architecture Exhibition with the emblematic title *Sensing the future. The architect as seismographer.*

With this installation they inquire into the logic of the *existenzminimum.*

> We have always been interested in the design of human motion and have had several successful collaborations with choreographers. In the early 90s, we were fascinated by motion-economy principles designed by efficiency engineers at the turn of the century that effectively redesigned the body as an extension of the factory apparatus. This notion was extended to housework, ostensibly to free the housewife from the home so that she could join the paid labor force. As we now know, the move toward efficiency ultimately led the housewife toward progressively more obsessive care of the home. In any case, we became interested in time-saving manuals for housework. We learned that in pressing a shirt, for example, a minimum of effort is used to reshape the shirt into a two dimensional, repetitive unit which consumes a minimum of space. The standardized ironing pattern always "disciplines" the shirt to a flat, rectangular shape which fits economically into orthogonal systems of storage: the shipping carton, the display case, the dresser drawer, the closet shelf, and the suitcase. When worn, the residue of the orthogonal logic of efficiency is registered on the surface of the body. The parallel creases and crisp, square corners of a clean, pressed shirt have become sought after emblems of refinement. We asked ourselves, what if the task of ironing could free itself from the aesthetics of efficiency altogether? Perhaps the effects of ironing could more aptly represent the postindustrial body through the image of the post functional. Thus, we developed labor-intensive patterns of ironing that produced shirts that could not be packed or stacked (D + S 2004).

On this territory, between 1921 and 1927, Man Ray created *Cadeau*, a ready-made work, using an iron and some nails. Ray's "present" proved to be paradoxical, like all Dadaist works. The tool for ironing is translated into an a-functional utensil or a tool that frays and wears out.

With this installation D + S interpret new spatial and compositional forms, creating incredible architectonic solutions from a standard element, amid organic figures and topological compositions, playing with a spatial interpretation of the fold and the surface as unimaginable as it is successful. Thus shirts rebel against the use of the press that uniforms them and they give an image of live material; Kiesler's words come to mind when, as the *"Endless House"* was being developed, he stated: "The house is a living body, not just a combination of dead materials. [...] The house is the skin of the human body" (Ragon 74).

Bad Press anticipates with extraordinary intuition the themes of the fold, which would be developed digitally from the middle of the 90s.

In 1993 Greg Lynn published the text *Folding in architecture* and raised the question of the enwrapping surface, which combines with complex non-Euclidean geometry and topological forms. *Folding* is space folded back, whose forms originate from computer algorithm processing. The surface, interpreted as a new field of processes, focuses the attention on a complex dimension in which the linguistic distinction between signified and signifier, internal and external, makes way for the open, continuous, changing, coextensive dimension of the fold. As the surface folds upon itself it becomes a field of deforming forces, in which limit and symbol, sign and function are integrated into its actual substance.

Departing from the identity of the post-industrial body expressed by Deleuze, D + S interpret the fold as a multiple, mutant surface. The surface is the place where events are written that modify the initial state of stasis. Like architecture, it is subjected to ruin by the lasting events that consume it; the body's surface, too, visualizes and registers the power that constitutes it.

Hidden levels always exist in the work of the American duo. In *Bad Press* they take up again the themes of the controlling society from Michel Foucault's *Discipline and punish* (1975). The French philosopher explains: "But the body is also directly immersed in a political field: power relations operate an immediate grasp on it, they invest it, brand it, train it, torment it, force it to do certain jobs, to participate in rituals and they demand signs from it" (Foucault 76).

D + S's shirts reveal the system of conventions we are subjected to,

which, like a strait-jacket, imprisons us.
The architects point out that the feature that best identifies the fold is mutability: "If something can be folded it can also be unfolded and refolded. The fold is susceptible to being forgotten. Whereas the crease may be an even more compulsive metaphor for it has a memory. The crease is a track, it has representative value and the nature of an inscription. While the fold implies reversibility, the crease is decisive" (D + S 94b).

PLYWOOD (KINNEY) HOUSE, *BRIARCLIFF MANOR, NEW YORK, 1981*

In this house the architects studied the sense of the window not as an opening towards the external world but towards the internal one.
The facade, marked by the regular rhythm of the openings, does not correspond to the distributional logic of the residence.
The house therefore experiences a discontinuous, disconnected relationship between internal and external.
The wall is 8 inches thick: the distance between the surface of our eyes and the back part of the brain.
In this project number and measurements also acquired meaning and metaphor.

3. Between inside and outside

3.1 The non-signifying window-module

From the 70s onwards, while the official culture in Europe was intent on seeking an architecture that would show how strong its foundations were (Piano and Rogers' *Centre Pompidou* was built in 1977), in America one of the themes architectural research most frequently dealt with was the house. Criticism of the Modernist model and the assumptions that over time had proved weak as regards their hypotheses, in a climate of social transformation led to new responses. In their research Robert Venturi and Colin Rowe tended towards the recovery of historic American models, combined with a Manierist impulse that included the vernacular. This reappraisal opened the way to the Post-modern and to studies on the single-family house. Yet in this climate the resulting methods proved to be extremely varied. Departing from the *wood-frame* construction with the *Trubek* and *Wislocki* houses, Robert Venturi sought the way of local tradition. Those who mainly depicted an alternative focus to the nostalgic re-proposal of traditional models, though veiled by ironic play of an intellectual matrix, were Eisenman, on the one hand, and Hejduk and Gehry, on the other. Eisenman began his research with Terragni's cube, steering it through rotations and compenetration of the structural grid, while Hejduk with his *Wall House,* ritualized the sense of inhabiting and broke down the enclosure, setting up a relation with the wall, with the passage between inside and out. But it was Gehry who, extending his house at Santa Monica in California in 1978, thwarted any attempt to codify. Corrugated iron, galvanized mesh, multi-layered wood panels, framework construction systems: tradition was dismantled, deformed, built-in.
In 1981 D + S created the *Plywood (Kinney) House.* With its 28
traditional shape, a parallelepiped with a double-sloped roof, it was invented as a series of sheets perforated by openings and reassembled as happens in the construction of simple solids (origami).

The budget of the *Plywood House* was set exactly by the insurance money recuperated after the owner's house burned down. The new house had to sit on the old foundation. The *Plywood House* dealt with standardized building elements in conflict. The regular pattern of stock windows fell in locations very inconvenient to the program and that conflict was registered in the facade (D + S 2004).

It was a great challenge. The pattern of the windows gave the house its rhythm. Attention to both constituent as well as logical and numeric aspects brought architecture back to being a transmittable discipline, interpreting the charismatic Hejduk's teaching method. The architects reconsidered the value of number which, as in Pythagoras' tradition, took on multiple meanings. The plywood was 8 inches thick: the distance between the surface of our eyes and the back part of the brain. Number and distance took on sense and metaphor, heralding the space of mystery and the absurd. The body enclosed the mind in a discontinuous process, thus this house showed itself in a disconnected, discontinuous relationship between internal and external. The logic of window distribution did not respond to the logic of functioning of the house. Hejduk points out: "This house explores the true nature of the window, not as an opening onto the external world, but as an opening into our internal nucleus" (Hejduk 84).

With *Splitting* in 1974 Gordon Matta Clark cut through a quintessential home, showing suggested, dreamlike, paradoxical spatiality. Matta Clark transcended the disciplinary limits of architecture with his work and showed its conceptual strength, in which a new space was introduced into the pre-existing structure.

D + S retrieved the memory of the traditional American constructions with *Plywood House*: a mask that includes a space denying the actual sense of its structuring. They play with the culture of Venturian Post-modern times, showing its limits with an apparent research on skin as a challenge for the interior. The interpretation of skin, which in Venturi was a quotation and the construction of a language easily understood by the collectivity, in D + S translated into a complex system: in their philosophy skin is the border, the limit, the threshold separating inside from outside, a sort of sensitive armour, the interface on which the sentiments of pain and pleasure are traced. In this apparently neutral project, they trace a route in which internal and external no longer communicate. A dialectic which some years later would announce a new research trend when, from the 90s onwards, digital systems would challenge the concepts of separation and delimitation.

Studying the literature dear to the American architects, Marcel Duchamp, in a rented apartment at 11 Rue Larrey in Paris, by chance found himself in an ambivalent situation which he later translated into a work: a really strange door, on hinges in a corner between two rooms, which closed and opened at the same time the bathroom and the bedroom. The door thus closed one room and simultaneously opened the other; always open and always closed. Things happen by chance without a doubt.

3.2 The virtual house

Diller and Scofidio designed the *Slow House* (1991) at North **32-33**
Haven on the coast of Long Island. The theme of the holiday home for a Japanese art dealer became, in the philosophy of the New York Studio, the departure point for experimentation that would bring back into play the actual essence of dwelling, of protection, of the property market in relation to the beauty of the site and the sea view. The commitment concerning the house was that for the client it had to be the place for negotiations on the art market.

The conceptual stance taken by the American duo is always of an etymological nature. They explain that 'to vacate' in Latin is rooted in the theme of travel. Tourism, the dominant theme of their work, in today's view takes on the loss of values linked with discovery and the sense of challenge or danger they used to contain. Nowadays we can travel virtually, staying still in our own home, via the internet or the numerous TV programs suggesting trips to unknown lands. In this project D + S took the research they had begun with the *Plywood House* project to its extreme limits.

In 1988, when the property market crash had brought on a crisis, Philip Johnson and Mark Wigley realised the now well-known *Deconstructivist Architecture* exhibition at the MoMA in New York, bringing together the most important design experiments, works mostly not realised, by Gehry, Eisenman, Tschumi, Koolhaas, Hadid and Coop Himme(l)blau. This exhibition was to cause a reverse tendency. The themes raised were disjunction, syntactic deconstruction, loss of centrality, disassembly and reassembly of spatiality which, having eliminated the academic, linguistic, ideological and geometric boundaries, reconfigured an

SLOW HOUSE, *NORTH HAVEN, NEW YORK, 1991*

The theme of the threshold and the window as a new limit to cross or territory to explore is placed at the center of the "Slow House" project, ideated as a viewing machine. A video-camera connected with a monitor placed in front of the single window of the house, mediates the view of the external world.

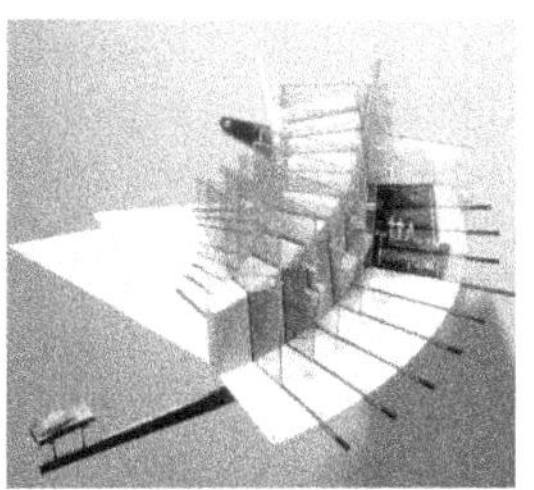

experimental territory which in the 90s would constitute the body of the IT and digital revolution.

> The Slow House was explicitly about visuality. The house is simply "a door that leads to a window that frames a view." In this design, we argued that the "picture window" may be seen as a higher technology in capturing a view than a video camera and monitor, as the video is encumbered by hardware and the window is not. The ultimate aspiration of high technologies, after all, is to purge the object and leave only effect (D + S 2004).

The theme of the threshold and the window as a new limit to cross or territory to explore is placed at the center of the *Slow House* project, ideated as a viewing machine.

In 1999 Terence Riley realised *The Un-Private House* exhibition and respective catalogue at the MoMA in New York, including the *Slow House* among the few projects not realized. D + S proposed three guidance systems in the spatial and organizational interpretation of the house: the car windscreen, television screen and the picture window.

The symbols of the capitalist and consumer society are the television and the automobile, two of the machines conventionally used as systems of flight. The house captures the effects of the two media, the automobile fleeing from the city towards the vacation house, and the video-camera which takes apart then recomposes the external image of the ocean on a video screen placed opposite the only window in the house. The house feels the effects of the slowing down process of the journey and the two main Kantian structures, time and space, are slowed down and crystallized. Ten years earlier, when digital systems had not yet revolutionized the conception of architectonic space, John Hejduk, speaking of *Plywood House*, put forward the theme of travel again: "We are embraced and suspended between entering and exiting, suspended in time and space" (Hejduk 84).

To travel and perceive space through the windscreen constitutes the moment of expectation, the non-linear route, the perception of the external world through a deformed, curved frame of what we are observing. The house undergoes this deforming effect of the optical and perspective cone, and curves following a pre-established angle of deformation; it does not have a main facade. As provocation or by vocation, it has a narrow frontage containing the entrance and indicating the route that forks to reach, up a gentle stairway, the large picture-window at the end of the *Slow House*. The narrow entrance is marked by a slab soaring outwards and creating a strong link with a performance designed by Vito Acconci in 1976: *The Board Room*. In Acconci's provocation the board stretches out of the window, an invitation that turns the metaphor into a disturbing physical presence. In the *Slow House*, on the other hand, the slab is an invitation to enter. As D + S point out, the house is a mechanism of optical stimulation which leads from the entrance to the only window placed at the end. Two icons are introduced here: the television, a symbol of technological culture, and the chimney, the nostalgic symbol of the pre-technological society. The window, the Renaissance visual frame which encloses the cut-out image of space of the territory, to the point of taming it, undergoes interference from the screen, connected to a video-camera. This is placed at the top of a column in line with the chimney stack and records the ocean on the monitor in a vacant, solitary dimension devoid of obstacles. The screen thus transmits a reality in real time, or recorded images on days with unstable weather conditions, determining an extreme filter and the rediscovery of electrical vision. Ultimately the monitor and the video-camera mediate the direct view of the external world.

From a conceptual viewpoint, the *Slow House* is the opposite of Mies van der Rohe's *Farnsworth*. The widespread transparency of the Miesian design showed the logic of "organ space" functioning and the internal-external reading process was reversible. With *Slow House* D + S highlight the temporal nature of the view and represent a new manifesto of information architecture. It is the landscape that discovers the inhabitant. The window no longer shows the outside from within but our actual interior. The bedrooms are situated on the lower floor, but the most complex part is developed on the higher floor with a section that slowly rises higher and higher showing the plan of functions contained in it.

After excavation and reinforcement to anchor it to the ground, as if bound by a vocation to last eternally, the house was not realised, due to the investor's financial collapse and the drop in interest for the art market. Duchamp followers and affected by the chance circumstances that haunted his works, basically this trouble decreed the fortune of the design, which remained forever virtual.

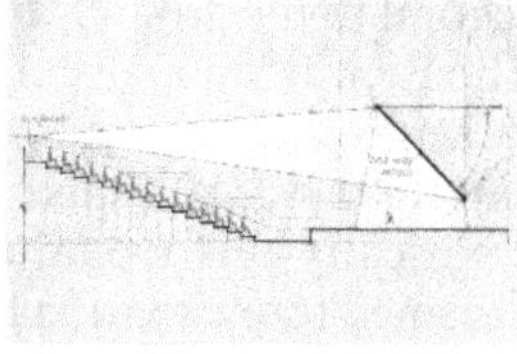

MOVING TARGET, *PALAIS DES BEAUX-ARTS, BRUSSELS, 1996*

They recuperate an extraordinary insight, realised in the installation Delay in Glass, *of a machine-device-flat surface rotated at 45°, a mirror reversing reality, the vertical-horizontal axes themselves, and the sense of physical gravity.*

Diller + Scofidio brought a new actor onto the scene, not visible but fundamental throughout the entire performance: a computer connected to a Mylar mirror with very high definition.
In conjunction with the video-projector, the mirror enabled new theater registers in which the dancers were freed from the confines of gravity, as the image in the mirror was reoriented by 90°, while the pre-recorded dancers were freed from the confines of bodily physics as their actions were produced through morphing technologies.

4. The worlds of reflection

4.1 Nijinski's diaries

The theater has always developed a narrow research trend aimed at formulating thought, at understanding our own times. When the dimension of the relationship subject/representation changed in modern times, the first extraordinary transformations of the theater space were born. In contrast with the Greek theater, which restored man to the center of the stage, in 1927 Gropius, with his *Total Theater* designed for the Berlin producer Erwin Piscator, revolutionized stage space. The circular proscenium, lowered and made to rotate 180° together with the stalls, was turned into an arena which wrapped round and encircled the audience. Spectators were immersed in a performance that became dynamic, inexorably modifying the point of observation and the perspectives that opened up. Not by chance was this project born following the musical discoveries in dodecaphonic music introduced by Schönberg in 1923. Between 1915 and 1920 Vienna was the complex node embracing the hub of development of contemporary art. Loos, Kokoschka, Schönberg, Webern and Kraus would meet at the Café Imperial. From these meetings the interpretations of architecture, art, music and literature were to originate that would give creative life-blood to the developments of the 1900s, and generate ground for continuous experimentation. But it was Frederick Kiesler that would astonish, with his work always linked with the theater, the place where the tragic sense of existence is played out and where fiction takes on the undisputed role of changing identity. The first version of *Endless Theater* belongs to 1923, where Kiesler introduced the concept of dynamism into theater scenography, with the aim of mixing actors and public in a new concept that abandoned the central, one-way public-show model. The introduction of the use of kinetic systems in the scenography for Karel Capek's play *R.U.R (Rossum's Universal Robots)* (Berlin 1923), with a moving stage and the possibility to see two people reflected in a mirror behind the stage, abandoned the distance of the performance, making it outdated.
How has the spectacle changed in the multimedia IT society?
The interaction between real time experience and images recorded by the media, according to D + S's way of thinking, has

modified the way we perceive events and social relations. Their investigation addresses everyday life to show artificiality. In their research D + S recuperate Artaud's theater of cruelty.

"Artaud wants to establish a state of existence of the body in which all influences, all that is natural and all that is cultural, are stripped from it so that it is itself, reduced to the essence, with no family, God or internal organs" (D + S in Teyssot 90).

In 1996 Diller + Scofidio arranged the theater spectacle *Moving* 36-37
Target with the Belgian group Charleroi/Danses, headed by the choreographer Frédéric Flamand and inaugurated at the Palais des Beaux Arts in Brussels.

For this event they retrieved the uncensored diaries of the ballet dancer Nijinski. The dancer's schizophrenic universe was used as a metaphor for investigation, in order to analyze the relationship between the normal and the pathological. Analyzed in art by Francis Bacon and in philosophy by Foucault and Deleuze, the schizophrenic lives in a deterritorialized, discontinuous dimension, without a will. His spiritual dimension is incoherent, unstable, unconciliatory.

In *Moving Target* D + S recuperated an extraordinary insight realized in the installation *Delay in glass*, of a machine-device-flat surface rotated at 45°, a mirror reversing reality, the vertical-horizontal axes themselves, and the sense of physical gravity.

Yes, these two pieces are cousins. We were always interested in the problem of "live" versus "mediated" experience in theater. Given our media-saturated world, contemporary culture presumes mediated experience to be of a lower order than authentic experience; mediated is considered qualitatively less than "live." This probably answers the question, "Why does the theater survive when audiences have access to many forms of mediated entertainment at the touch of a button?" As architects in the theater, we accept that liveness has appeal but the gray areas of mediation are more interesting especially because audiences today are equipped to deal with multiple registers of information. *Delay in Glass* cut the stage in half. The audience had an unimpeded view of the downstage half. The upstage half was blocked from direct view and could only be seen via a 45° mirror overhead. This *interscenium* (as opposed to proscenium) produced new rules for the narrative space of the stage. *Moving Target* went one step further. The 45° mirror in conjunction with video projection allowed for a new choreography where live and pre-recorded dancers could merge spatially in an impossible space enjoying new forms of hyper virtuosity: live dancers are freed from the confines of gravity as the mirror reorients everything by 90°, the pre-recorded dancers are freed from the confines of bodily physics as their actions are produced through morphing technologies (D + S 2004).

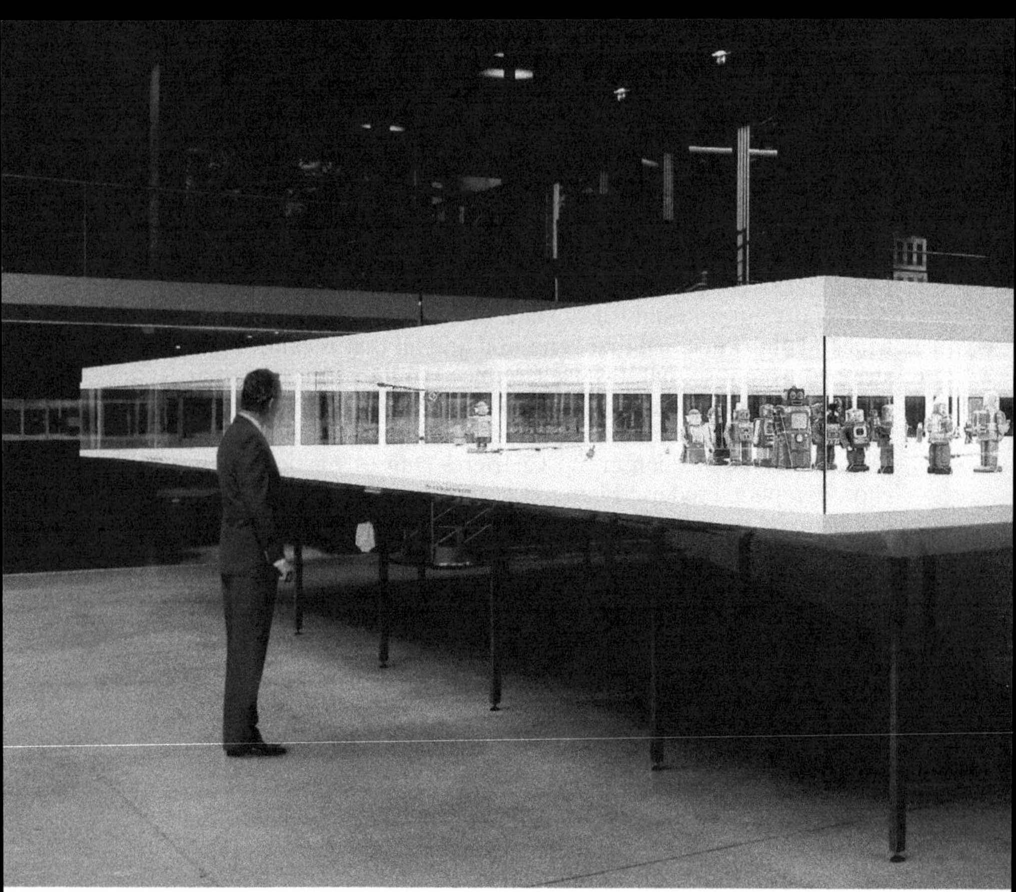

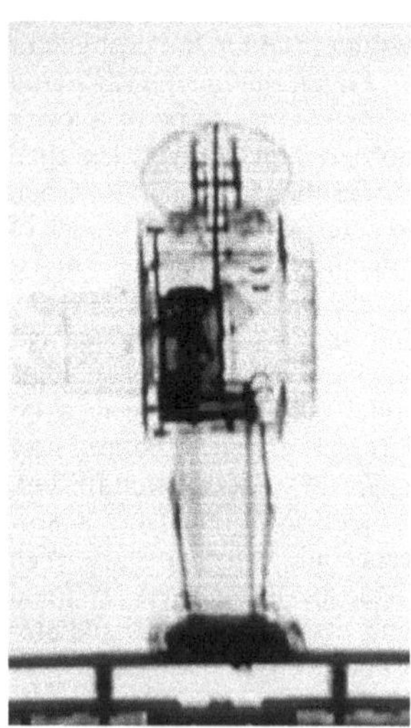

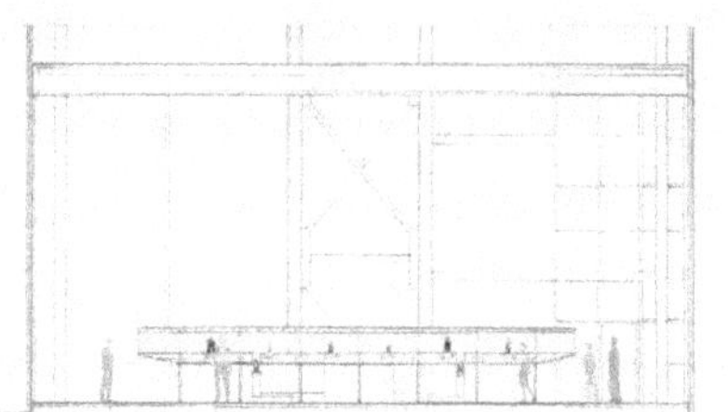

MASTER/SLAVE, *FONDATION CARTIER, PARIS, 1999*

Rolf Fehlbaum's collection of toy robots is displayed at Nouvel's large gallery.
D + S interpret the robot culturally, through cinematography that has inverted the master/slave relationship.
In their installation the observer is turned into an inspector.

The architects brought a new actor onto the scene, not visible but fundamental throughout the entire performance: a computer connected to the Mylar mirror with very high definition and a reflective capacity of 99.8%.
They found themselves faced with a problem typical of mirrors, namely that of generating a double reflection. They used this limit to project video images onto the stage and generate a hybrid space which, as the architects point out, was neither stage nor screen but both. In an interview with Laurie Anderson D + S reveal the backstage activity. Using a system of optical tracks borrowed from Gulf War technology, the computer drew a series of virtual cages on the screen via a system of sensors linked with the color of the dancers' costumes, and followed the movement of the dancers, drawing diagrams in real time of the powerful lines the dancers traced on the stage.
The stage became interactive and the computer visualized the fields of force reversed in terms of plane and direction, eliminating the perspective view in a profoundly virtual plane that combined real and reflected figures. This parallel environment included the spectator, showing him the spectacular truth of fiction. The reflecting machine shows a reality that the spectator would not otherwise perceive: it is the space hidden, evoked, virtual, mnemonic, the space beyond the stage. During the show, a commercial for an unreal pharmaceutical company called Normal, whose products treat the illnesses of a post-psychoanalytic culture, served as an interlude.
D + S ask themselves and the public about the sense of the normal and the pathological, making fun of 20th century normalization. They break with the traditional, conventional mono-focal theater structure, which converges in the static place of the stage. The Post-modern, electronic body is reconfigured through a mirror that virtually projects real space and video installations in mediated time (real or delayed). The purpose is to fraction the perceptive unity of the public, and enable a reading that involves several levels and scenes. The interactive technology highlights the worlds surrounding us without censor, destabilizing the passive eye and involving the mind's eye.

4.2 Deferred time

When Walter Benjamin published *The work of art in the age of mechanical reproduction* in 1936 he identified a double paradigm in the creative process, *hic et nunc* (here and now), which characterized the uniqueness of the artistic act. The work of art was fixed in a definite time and place. Nowadays technics have been replaced by technology which, with its etymology in *tecne + logos,* has taken on a greater degree of complexity. Information technology is endowed with thought, thought which is more and more active in transforming reality. The spaces generated by the digital paradigm challenge the concepts of place and territory, creating a space devoid of scale, continuous and fluid. In 1984 the American novelist William Gibson coined the term *Cyberspace* for the first time in the novel *Neuromancer.* In his interpretation, as in all literature of this genre, this new environment, where time and space do not exist, is controlled by the power of multinationals through information networks, the place where all virtual travelers meet. We are witnessing phenomena today that are increasingly active in connecting architecture to the media, and the surface becomes the place of information exchange. D + S pay great attention to the theme of media architecture. They outline and identify two cultural attitudes that highlight two parallel diseases: technophilia and technophobia.

> The last decade was full of extremes from both camps. The technophiles euphorically predicted that technologies would eliminate the conventional need for travel, sex, and even space. The technophobes bemoaned those losses. We have gotten past the reductive rhetoric of the 90s and are able to integrate technologies freely into the arts (D + S 2004).

The two techno-extremes, the architects point out, are attracted by live radio-television, the *liveness* dimension which captures images in real time. Technophobes are attracted by the aura of the real experience, recorded while the fact is happening, while technophiles see in it "the technological ability to simulate reality". Real time translates into immediate time which, via digital techniques and computational speed, allows reality to be grasped *live,* as it is happening, without censor or cuts.
"Real time records without control and turns the observer into an eye witness".

JET LAG, *LANTAREN THEATER, ROTTERDAM, DUTCH ELECTRONIC ARTS FESTIVAL, 1998*

A multi-media theater work with the collaboration of Builders Association. In Jet Lag they came up with two real stories, contradictory and filled with the human restlessness of our times, from which they developed a cinematic narrative. The characters on stage are freed from the conventions of time and space.
In this work Diller & Scofidio sought new spatial rules of the stage. The first story told of Sarah Krassnoff, who crossed the Atlantic no less than 167 times in a period of six months in 1970 with a series of New York - Amsterdam, Amsterdam - New York flights. The American grandmother was trying to save her grandson from being pursued by his father and the child's psychiatrist.
The second event D + S drew attention to was the famous one of the yachtsman Donald Crowhurst, who took part in 1969, without proper athletic preparation, in a round-the-world yacht sail. Following his first real problems, Crowhurst decided to circle the shores of South America following the coastline. The London Sunday Times reported the fake tales of the trip and fake geographical positions as true, as if his journey were progressing. The architects highlighted the role media technology played in the existence of these characters. Their intention was to show the media as a new subject on the stage.

"However", D + S remark, "whether motivated by the desire to conserve the real or invent it artificially, the live broadcast is synonymous with real and the real is an object of acritical desire for both techno-extremes" (D + S in Pongratz - Perbellini 2000).

One of the techno-sceptical philosophers, Jean Baudrillard, raised the issue of tele-reality in *The perfect crime. Has television killed reality?*. The French philosopher points out: "At the height of technological performances the irresistible impression remains that something is missing – not because we have lost it (the real), but because of the fact that we are no longer able to see it: that is, the fact that it is no longer us who prevail over the world, but the world that prevails over us" (Baudrillard 96).

D + S have always used video-cameras, computers or webcams in their work, with the intent to sabotage the distinction between direct or mediated experience, to the point of making it collapse once and for all. For them, technology linked with the media enables reality to be unmasked, to be shown bare, and a contingent or parallel truth to be grasped, while simultaneously revealing the diseases the system suffers from, and disclosing the actual mechanisms of control, so as to make them public.

They tackle the theme of media architecture with a performance in which they expose the ubiquitous nature of surveillance technologies. In their work they clarify the passage from the control system to that of security, nowadays partly accepted
49 socially. *Jump Cuts* was realized in 1995 at the United Artists Cineplex Theater (San Jose, California). The space of the lobby was used criss-crossed by escalators, which were equipped with television cameras recording the public live. A system of 12 TV cameras recorded from above to below and another 12 from below to above. The images were transmitted and projected outside on a series of video display screens mounted on the facade overlooking the street, causing, as the artists stated, "electronic turning inside-out of the building". D + S interpreted the implications of transparency, far from the principles that inspired modern architecture; when glass is made translucent the view from inside is blocked and a video surrogate replaces it.

The architects explain: "The presence of the video-cameras and screens arouses the public and leads them to perform for the television cameras, reversing the place of the spectacle from the theater to the lobby" (Betsky 2003).

In their projects on video surveillance D + S show how reality and fiction are interchangeable.
While *Jump Cuts* endeavors to generate a sort of social art, in *Jet* 44-45
Lag they came up with two real stories, contradictory ones filled with the human restlessness of our times, from which they developed a cinematic narrative.

We have too much respect for the craft and complexity of filmmaking to make easy parallels between film and the cinematic use of space. We are interested, however, in new ways to construct narrative. This shows up in our multi-media work. *Jet Lag*, which we conceived and co-directed, weaves two unrelated narratives together about characters freed from the conventions of space and time. *Jet Lag* was also driven by the desire to invert the spatial rules of stage and screen. Regarding cinematic works, we are interested in Stanley Kubrick's body of work that attempted to try every genre .... from war epic, to political satire, to thriller, to romance. My dream (Diller) is to one day make a feature film (D + S 2004).

It was the high existential content expressed by the two stories described in *Jet Lag* that intrigued and bewitched the American duo, so much so that they translated them into a video spectacle lasting 80 minutes, presented in 1998 at the Lantaren Theater in Rotterdam for the Dutch Electronic Art Festival.
In 1970 Sarah Krassnoff crossed the Atlantic no less than 167 times in a period of six months, with a series of New York - Amsterdam, Amsterdam - New York flights. The American grandmother was trying to save her grandson from being pursued by his father and the child's psychiatrist. After the exhausting chase Ms Krassnoff died of jet lag. In his book *The third window* Paul Virilio explained that Sarah Krassnoff was "a contemporary heroine who lived in deferred time". The paradoxical aspect was that the real characters spent their time at airports, which according to Marc Augé epitomize the idea of contemporary space where the specificities of places are lacking. On this journey no territory existed except the one tragically experienced in the story.
The second event D + S drew attention to was the famous one of the yachtsman Donald Crowhurst, who took part in 1969, without proper athletic preparation, in a round-the-world yacht sail. Following his first real problems, Crowhurst decided to circle the shores of South America following the coastline. The London

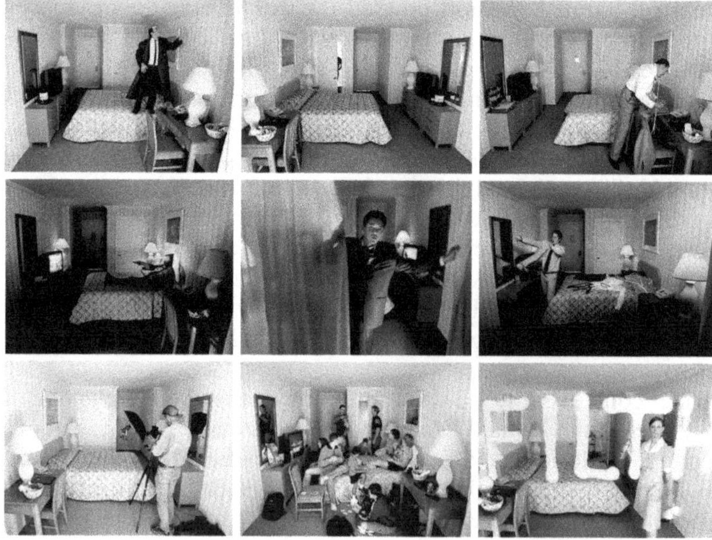
FILT

JUMP CUTS, *UNITED ARTISTS CINEPLEX THEATER, SAN JOSE, CALIFORNIA, 1995*

A system of 12 TV cameras recorded from above to below and another 12 from below to above. The images were transmitted and projected outside on a series of video display screens mounted on the facade overlooking the street.

On the opposite page:
FACSIMILE, *MOSCONE CONVENTION CENTER WEST, SAN FRANCISCO, 2004*

Sunday Times, which had sponsored the boat, equipping it with video cameras provided by the BBC so that he could record his journey, reported the fake tales of the trip and fake geographical positions as true, as if his journey were progressing. While the media provided precise coordinates, the navigator drifted in a confused public space.

D + S worked on this theater piece to reveal the role media technology played in the daily existence of these personalities. The media turned out to be the new subject on the stage.

The architects highlight the new dimension of our times, no longer Benjamin's here and now but a geography in which time and space are deferred: a simulated geography, but not for that less true. In the era of information and telematic networks, where private becomes a collective I, the two stories show an opposite and coinciding dimension. In the first story the grandmother's fear was being seen or found, whereas in the second the desire is exactly to place oneself at the center of attention, to be seen, to the point of overriding the norm, to such an extent as to simulate reality, make it virtual or potential. The architects' reflection aims to disclose false appearances: the apparently controlled space of the airport and the apparently free space of the ocean undergo disjunction. D + S have always singled out almost a line of demarcation where reality splits, to the point of becoming multiple. Virtual indicates a dimension of oblivion, non-coincidence, a state of non-consciousness: the new code of the mediatized body, ever less programmable.

5. Connective architecture

5. The society of control

Orwell's novel *1984* first analyzed the media surveillance system that involved and demarcated the post-industrial society. Prophetic, visionary and lucid, the author identified a control machine in *Big Brother* without precedent in history.

In *The electronic eye. The rise of surveillance society* David Lyon writes: "Closed circuit television cameras, credit cards, cash dispensers, magnetic identity cards, cross checks on personal data between different types of archives, mobile phones and call identifiers, invisible checks on productivity [...] The novelty lies in the "digital self", a sort of electronic double composed of the "sensitive" data of flesh and blood individuals, sold and exchanged between the numerous government and private databases, used to grant bank credit and loans and decisive in orienting the single individual's life expectations. They are thus electronic identities that travel autonomously and intangibly along dedicated networks" (Lyon 97).

This dimension, today extensive and uncontrollable, had an amazing forerunner in the system of construction of the labyrinth which, according to the historian Philochorus (270 BCE), was for the Cretans a prison in which the only evil was being closely watched over.

Whereas the labyrinth etymologically designates a set of subterranean galleries, in the period 1830-40 Bentham's *Panopticon* program denoted a circular architectonic figure in the center of which a tower perforated by large windows enabled the prisoners and their cells to be observed at any point. According to Foucault, who dedicated a great deal of space to the theme of surveillance in *Discipline and punish*, the machine-prison indicates the control system of the power contemporary society descends from and depends on. D + S devote a focal area of research to this theme in their work.

In 1999 they realized the installation *Master/Slave* embodying **40-41**
metaphor, amusement, references to science fiction cinema and the theme of the mechanical body endowed with a soul; in this work a collection of toy robots were visualized.

They were arranged on a conveyor belt in a bureaucratic situation,

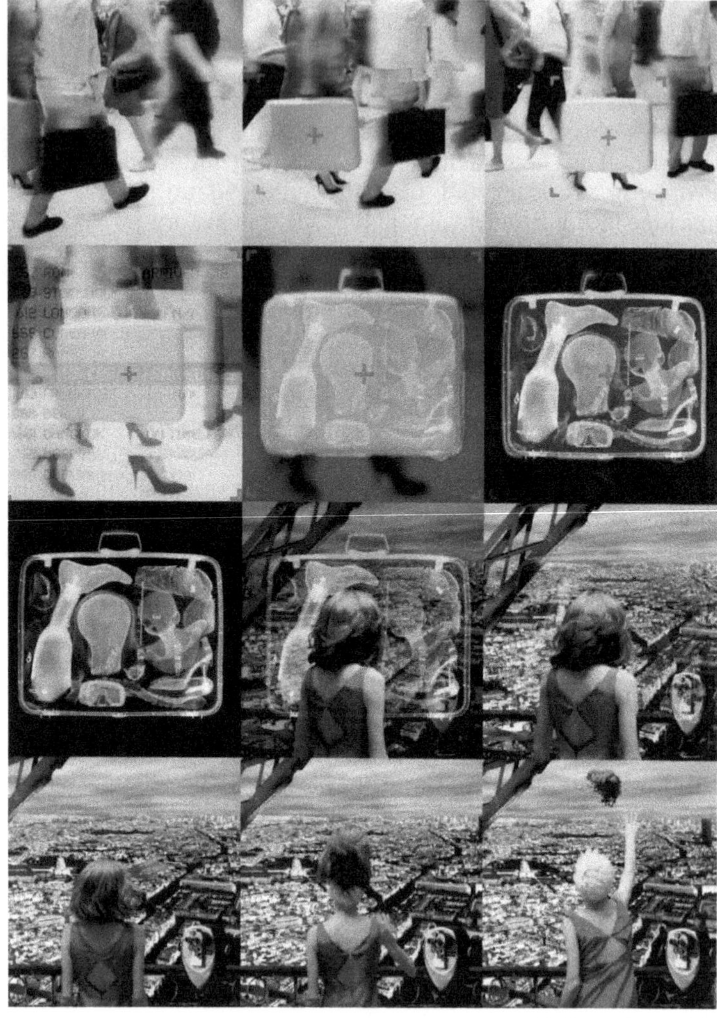

TRAVELOGUES, *INTERNATIONAL ARRIVALS TERMINAL, JFK INTERNATIONAL AIRPORT, NEW YORK, 2001*

The installation Travelogue was composed of 33 lenticular screens arranged along the entire length of the corridor: a system of display-images each lasting two seconds, which added up to a short movie as one passed through. At the airport the suitcases being X-rayed became the place of security control.

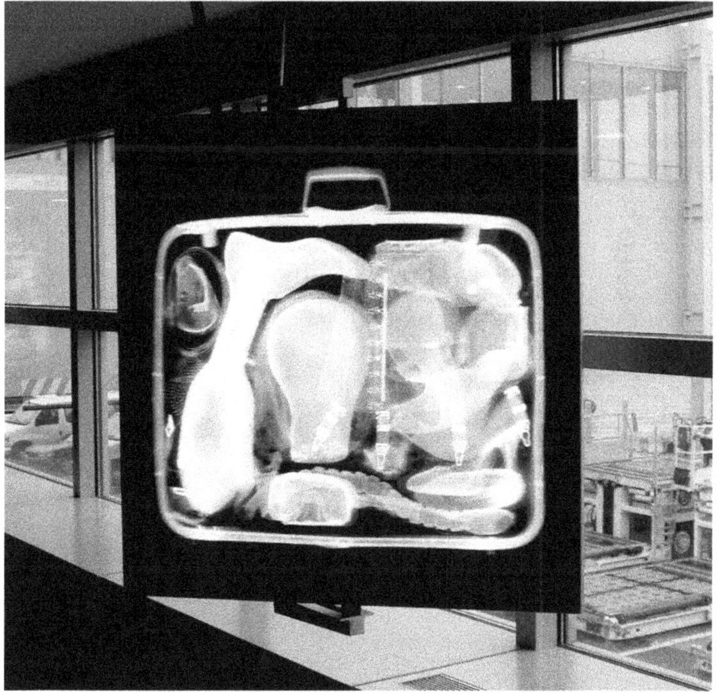

subjected to a careful albeit invasive surveillance, safety and control system.

In the context of a science fiction exhibition, the Cartier asked us to put Rolf Fehlbaum's collection of toy robots on display in the large glass gallery by Jean Nouvel. We had to first contemplate the robot culturally. In the Modernist imagination, the robot served as a surrogate body that could perform menial tasks and leave man free for more important activities. The utopian fantasy turned dystopian in popular film when the robot acquired enough artificial intelligence to invert the master/slave relationship. While Fehlbaum's robots were merely toys in the service of children, here, as museological artifacts they could set the rules of engagement (D + S 2004).

What made the installation so interesting, apart from the system of social-philosophical relations the work possesses, was the built architecture, the space within which the toy robots moved - almost an imploded architecture reminiscent of Modernism which, placed at the spectators' eye level, encouraged them to observe and judge.

The collection of toy robots inhabited a giant vitrine, not unlike the gallery in which it sat. It was, however, relentlessly horizontal and fluorescently-overlit and elevated to eye level on a grid of columns. Spectators were trapped between the glass boxes, and inadvertently were turned into inspectors. The colony of robots paraded on a 300-foot long conveyor system. Along the travel route, the robots were made to form lines and then they were released arbitrarily, not unlike an unemployment office. The only labor the robots were expected to perform was to pose before live cameras, identify themselves, avail themselves to the scrutiny of medical devices (an airport scanner was at the base of the down ramp). The surveillance system displayed details of the robots at key moments (D + S 2004).

The architectonic and spatial component of this project is vigorously represented, as in the great models used on film sets, and leads the observer to enter the world the irreverent duo are exploring. In their work irony is a system to reflect and gain awareness of an increasingly capillary condition of surveillance and control to which we are all usually subjected, in a more or less aware manner. In this overturning of roles and identity D + S give us the key to understanding the new, more and more complex scenarios of the information society.

5.2 Screens and displays

In the 60s Marshall McLuhan was one of the first to sense the revolution underway that digital systems would introduce: "In the mechanical era we had extended our bodies into space. Nowadays, after more than a century of electrical technology, we have actually extended our central nervous system into a global embrace which abolishes space and time" (McLuhan 64).

In 1969 Rob Stern highlighted two trends or cultural attitudes in American architecture in *New Directions in American Architecture*: an exclusive one, operating under the Purist and orthodox conception of the Modern tradition, and an inclusive one under the influence of the media.

Obviously, the signs of change in architecture, both spatial and conceptual, were born in the 1900s in that transformation of the facade and its actual skin. With the invention of neon lights and intermittent LED lighting advertising was introduced into the city, beginning with the great capitals of the world, Paris, Berlin, London and New York: sequences of words proclaiming the production of goods, with communicativeness and symbolism creating a new aesthetic of visual communication.

From the first decades of the 1900s onwards, in expressionist Berlin the first speaking architecture was born, in the form of the *Lichtarchitektur* that decreed the birth of modern architecture. Mendelsohn was the architect who anticipated communication architecture, with a 20-metre high screen in his *Columbus Haus* department store design. This new tendency encouraged the critics of the time to devise a new slogan: *Reklame Architektur*.

From the 60s onwards, with the predominance of goods in the consumer society, this tendency became increasingly fervent, so much so as to establish itself as an authentic publicity message.

D + S embodied the new information frontier *par excellence*. In their work they made visible the technologies of desire and the rituals of buying and selling, which they had explored in the installation *Soft Sell*, realized in 1993 on 42nd Street in Times Square. On this New York street, famous for its movie theaters, shops, restaurants and porno shops, a sort of general market, the American duo interpreted the culture of the monitor and publicity, realizing a parody of messages aimed at promoting unattainable desires. Two giant female lips emitted messages to passers-by in sensual, persuasive tones. The act of displaying

clearly distinguishes our times and D + S display displaying, in the places appropriate to carry out these functions, provoking public reaction. Paradox is basically the weapon that enables the mechanism to be revealed. Their art is political as were the Dada provocations at the dawning of the 20th century.
Today we are witnessing the birth of multimedia, IT architectures, bearing increasingly complex messages, which capture and send back global images in real time, generating new flows of information between the observer and the facade-screen. D + S were among the first to understand the language of the media and how the media modified the concept of space itself. They used screens and displays with the purpose of placing the power watching us under surveillance, and disclosing the very processes involving information, operating without censorship. In their work we see the evolution from the 80s to halfway through the 90s in the use of technological systems. Whereas in the first installations the display was a sort of closed circuit monitor, when IT transformed the monitor into an interface, the computer became increasingly present and modified the messages themselves. D + S considered screens as overturned planes, both in meaning and perspective, as in two different works realized in 1995: *Indigestion* and *Cold War*.

> **61** We made *Indigestion* at a time when interactivity rearranged the rules of art practice by limiting the authority of the artist while promising limitless freedoms to the viewer. This was always disingenuous. The piece was meant to aesthetically demonstrate the limitations of control built into software by the artist for the viewer. *Indigestion* condenses an archetypal film noir narrative into a terse exchange between two characters of ambiguous relation across a dinner table. Choice is offered to lure the subject into an interrogation of reductive binaries such as masculine/feminine, high class/low class, fact/fiction, and real/virtual. The video consists of a dining scene projected onto a horizontal screen/table. A nearby touch screen offers character replacements from a variety of gender and class stereotypes. The food type follows. The narrative remains continuous at any switch point though nuanced by differences of character. This work was seen as very politically incorrect and had a short life in the U.S.. It did better in Europe and Asia (D + S 2004).

The table is turned into a screen here, whereas in Florida they transformed the arena into a great display. In their philosophy the message is used as a way to rouse the observer from a condition of passive acceptance and, at the same time, highlight the autonomy of public art and its capacity to grant new cultural layers to the site.

> Like institutionalized warfare, hockey, like many field sports and board games, is part of the culture of conquest with highly developed codes of propriety and hostility. The installation used the ice field as a video projection screen fed by a grid of networked video projectors overhead. In a series of videos that exploited the unusual size and orientation of the video image, *Cold War* was meant to foil the expectations of a captive audience perched to witness a sporting event and introduce, instead, a cultural framework of "battle" within which to consider the event to follow (D + S 2004).

As Derrick de Kerckhove points out in his vibrant essay *The architecture of intelligence*, the passage from the α-principle to the ε-principle determined the great revolution from written to electric language. If printed paper represented one of the greatest triumphs of the 1450s, the media image has inexorably crushed the concept itself of writing and space-time sequence.

The phenomenon of the *media building* – buildings transformed into interactive screens – has been explored best by Paul Virilio, the philosopher-urbanist. He clarifies the passage from the archaic societies which expressed the values of the mass to the modern one which channeled the energy of the internal combustion engine and electricity into mechanical production in industry, then to the contemporary one, which acts on the third dimension of matter: information, the synthesis of electricity, electronics and informatics. This third dimension "enables information or images to be transmitted at the speed of light" (Virilio 2000). The image, the philosopher points out, is the most economic type of information that exists.

In 1997 D + S were invited by the San Francisco Public Arts 48
Commission to participate with a public work of art for the Moscone Convention Center.

> The project began with the paradox of being asked to make a public art work for the new Moscone expansion, a building that was neither open to the public nor that left any sizable public space on its footprint. By default, the site for the work became the outer surface of the building facade (D + S 2004).

They created a flat screen 16 feet high and 27 feet wide, supported by apparatus. A video camera, connected to the back of the monitor, broadcast live. The architects communicated to the "public" in the street the idea of the scanner that enables enlargement, deforming the image like a magnifying-glass does.

BRASSERIE, *SEAGRAM BUILDING, NEW YORK, 2000*

Philip Johnson had built a restaurant in the underground space of the tower in 1959; following a fire in 1995 it was closed to the public. In the Brasserie *the architects handled the theme of vision. The restaurant was situated in the basement of the tower, completely lacking in light. Diller + Scofidio introduced electronic transparency: the sliding-door broadcast the image of the unaware client by video-camera on a series of 15 monitors placed in the bar area.*

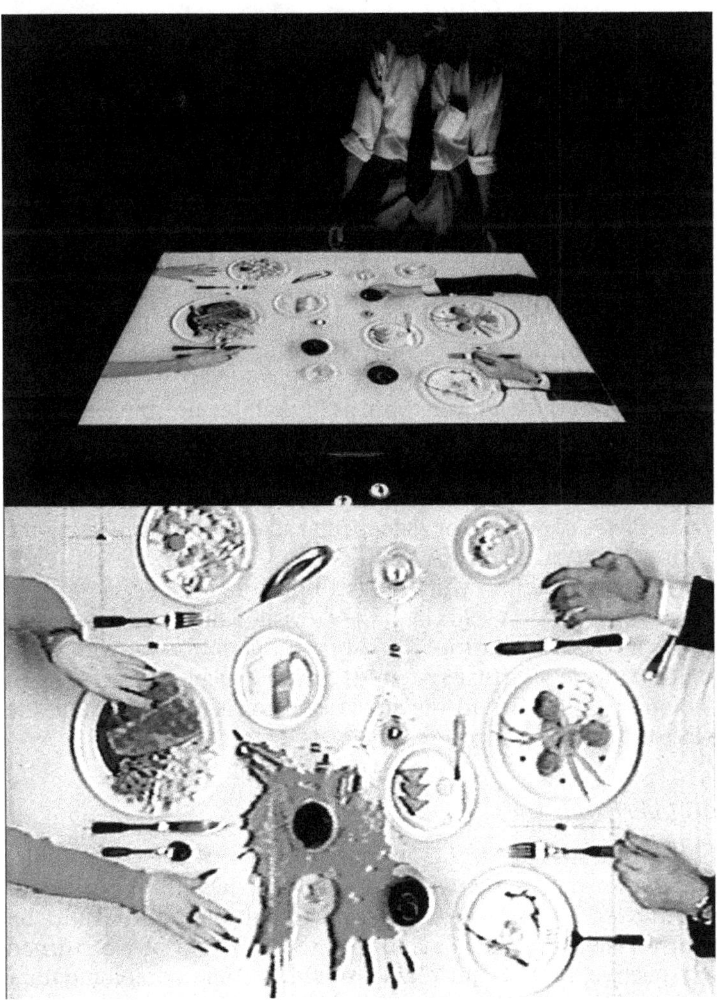

INDIGESTION, *PALAIS DES BEAUX-ARTS, BRUSSELS, 1995*

Indigestion *shows a film noir narrative of two people who are dining at a dining table. The observer may wonder about the reductive binaries such as masculine/feminine, high class/low class, fact/fiction, and real/virtual.*
A nearby touch screen enables by interaction the replacement of the characters represented from a variety of gender and class stereotypes while the narrative remains continuous at any switch point.

The structure moved slowly on rails connected to the parapet and ceiling, reversing the direction each time it reached the limit on one side. From the street the interior of the museum was observed, but the movement caused the large screen to enter a sort of closed circuit, showing deceptive images of imaginary characters placed in fictional spaces and, thanks to a television camera positioned above, views of the city. D + S staged the paradox between public art and private space. The two worlds, internal-external, experienced different messages. In their communication the image was always critical and complex, denying vision of the homogeneous and the globally indistinct. They proposed an imitation of reality, realizing a hyper-surface, an interface between the real and the virtual.

But if *media buildings* were born as IT architecture, the New York Studio has often worked to resemanticize ordinary or hybrid spaces like that of the corridor for International arrivals at JFK Airport in New York. In 2001 they realized the installation
52-53 *Travelogues*, composed of 33 lenticular screens arranged along the entire length of the corridor: a system of display-images each lasting two seconds, which added up to a short movie as one passed through. Ten years later they revisited the travel theme, but while in the installation *Tourisms: suitCase Studies* the open suitcases were a virtual system to travel through a geography of the mind, at the airport the suitcases being X-rayed became the place of security control.

5.3 Lunch with Mies

Guy-Ernest Debord, the greatest theorist of the Situationist International, foresaw with extraordinary lucidity in his book-manifesto *Society of the spectacle* that the real would be transformed into images and that in the world of overturned perspective, fiction and reality would become complementary planes. The spectacle dimension upsets the concept of real experience in favor of the predominance of the media. Several years later, Diller and Scofidio, in a society structured and "controlled" by the media, again put forward themes linked with social behavior in physical space.

Already in the 60s, Andy Warhol had undertaken an investigation into 'reading' the consumer society. The spectacle as an event was the focus of an experiment aimed at grasping unexpected moments of an everyday life which, captured by his camera, showed the subject as an actor on the stage. With Warhol the concept itself of sequence and writing changes. The American artist would phone his secretary in the morning to report on the previous day and she would write up his diary, consisting of quick accounts and notes on everyday life experiences. Writing also undergoes a mediation process. His famous sentence that in a near future everyone will have fifteen minutes of fame was to prove prophetic.

At Mies van der Rohe's *Seagram Building* in New York's Park Avenue, one of the symbols of American rationalist architecture, Elizabeth Diller and Ricardo Scofidio redesigned the *Brasserie* in **56-57**
2000. Philip Johnson had built a restaurant in the underground space of the tower in 1959; following a fire in 1995 it was closed to the public. In the *Brasserie* the architects handled the theme of vision. Mies' tidy space was reinterpreted, respecting divisions and alignments and proposing an installation-restaurant like an island within the rationalist space. The plan was organized around elementary functions, while space perception was highly effective.

> The Brasserie, originally designed by Philip Johnson, sits in the great icon of 20th Century glass and steel architecture, yet it is situated in its base, the only space in the building without light or visibility. That irony in this space of the Miesian unconscious launched the project. As glass could never perform according to modernist intentions in this space, we have reintroduced it in a post-Miesian way: "remnant" glass leaning against the wall for example is used as structure to precariously hold 25 seated diners. The missing connection between street and interior is made electronically. A pinhole camera lodged through the stone base and facing the street becomes a virtual window at the plasma screen just inside. A camera triggered by patrons arriving through the revolving door broadcasts the dynamic portrait of each successive patron entering onto a monitor over the bar (D + S 2004).

The unaware patron was shown on a series of 15 monitors placed above the counter in the bar area and overseen to the amusement of the patrons watching inside.

In *The perfect crime* Jean Baudrillard writes about the society animated by the virtual: "You live your life in real time – live and suffer directly on the screen. You think in real time – your thoughts are immediately codified by the computer. Have your revolution in real time – not in the street, but in the recording studio. You have your love affair in real time – with the video participating in its entire duration. Penetrate your body in real time – by video-endoscopy – your blood flow, your insides, as if you were there" (Baudrillard 96).

D + S channeled their energies from years of experimenting into the *Brasserie.* In *Para-Site* they had realized an installation like a foreign body inside the institutional place of the museum; in this project they take up some of the themes explored, from the use of television cameras to the prosthetic design of the dining room. It is still the theme of control and the spectacle, somewhere between voyeurism and activation of sensory factors.

> Dining in most international cities is a mixture of culinary pleasure and the theatrics of watching and being seen. This grand entry at the *Brasserie* is first announced electronically and is completed by a descent down the attenuated glass stair/runway, leaving the patron in the middle of the dining room (D + S 2004).

60 From the lobby the glass stairway leads into the dining room space and the patron enters the theater space as if on a catwalk. Like a self-supported display cabinet, modulated by ruby-colored, curved wooden strips reminiscent of Aalto's experiments in the Finnish pavilion created in New York in 1939, this environment, with its play of openings and closures, recalls the multimedia installations realized in places permeated by history. The wooden waves of the restaurant make the space rise and fall, at the same time, granting it its identity. D + S almost revisit the theme of travel with this environment, which resounds of transatlantic liner restaurants. The functional act of eating is re-codified as a collective ritual, a scenic spectacle that sets all the senses in motion. The interactive multimedia installation *Indigestion* (1995) comes to mind, realized by projecting a video onto a screen/table. The observer interacts using a touch screen, changing the characters shown and choosing between a variety of gender and class stereotypes, while the narration remains unchanged. D + S' video shows a situation of piles of food and drink rolling onto a tablecloth where the food ritual is represented as a fight between survival and struggle.

Just as the installation opens the way to interactivity between the observer and the work, so the space of the *Brasserie* seeks visual, tactile and perceptive interaction with the patron.

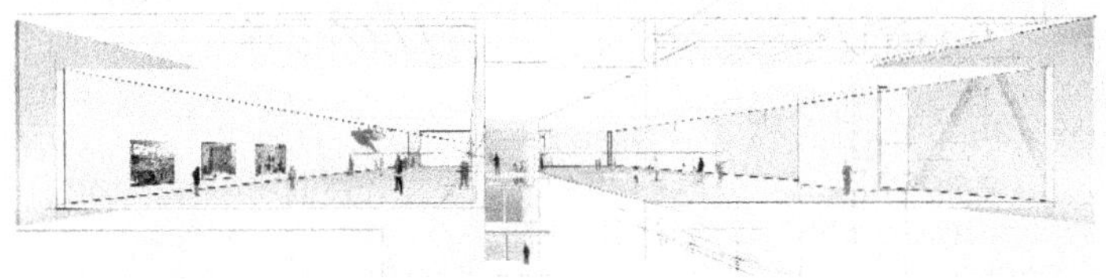

INSTITUTE OF CONTEMPORARY ART, *BOSTON, 2006*

In an extraordinary interview Rem Koolhaas had with Philip Johnson, when speaking of the *Brasserie* intervention the New York architect pointed out: "Elizabeth Diller said that 'architecture is a collection of special effects'".
The bar space is stimulating, the chairs in light-colored vinyl contain a gel used in the medical field under their plastic surface and recall places in clinics and the visual shock themes dear to the American duo. Every detail, from the bottles placed horizontally, almost as if to form a strange digital sequence, to the interesting work *Outcast,* signed by D + S and placed in the small room, is taken care of as in performance art. *Outcast* is composed of a piece of convex glass 15 meters long which contains blurred squares that can only be read if you observe them perpendicularly. Icons and airport signs appear, in a construction game like those Marc Augé describes in his text *Non places*, spaces where each of us basically feels at home. The issue of blurring the image links up with the studies on anamorphosis or mirror curvatures and, some time later, was to clarify the interest the two architects had in things that are not distinct and evade our capacity to see.
In this space of continuous referring back and concatenations of concepts the architects reawaken the observer by activating new critical processes.

5.4 Digital waterfront

The land and specificity of place may have determined for many thousands of years the dimension of architecture to the point of claiming physical belonging to it, but water is the natural element that best expresses the digital revolution. The new digital matter does not produce a direct imitation of natural liquids, so much as a liquefaction of the impenetrable mass that had characterized the first technological era. From halfway through the 90s onwards the projects that had a strong impact on international architectural culture were those that found a new dimension in water, re-reading the actual concepts of resistance, territory, structure and information. With this matter the most destabilizing element is included in the project, the one that brings back to mind archetypal scenarios of a primeval journey: suffice it to think of the Lars Spuybroek's *Sweetwater* (NOX) and Kas Oosterhuis' *Saltwater* pavilions, between the electronic and the primeval.

Liquid architecture is not only a philosophical principle, the architecture of pixels and flows, but a metaphorical principle and one of reference; suffice it to reread the projects that tackle the sea-front and have decreed the fortune of these interventions.

When the competition for the new *Institute of Contemporary Art* 65
on Fan Pier south of Boston was published in 2001, D + S Studio's idea won, where they handled the changing, unpredictable view of the *waterfront.* The desire was to create a museum that was contemporary but could express both the public and private image of a *Kunsthalle* at the same time.

The design proved innovative with references directed at interpreting the harbor landscape. A theater on the sea and an impressive overhang structure communicated a strong public image, but the entire perceptive system of the museum users was directed at the water, almost to the point of falling in. The museum program required by the competition announcement appeared extremely intricate: exhibition spaces, theater and media library, bookstore, shops and a restaurant.

D + S proposed an emblematic place, which altered the *waterfront* and generated a construction that reconsidered and challenged the traditional means with which architecture gives shape to its symbols. They explored the resources of the new digital technologies, modeling a new scenario for Boston. The museum translates into a virtual, diaphanous, fleeting image and suffers from certain sensations recalling constructivism and futurism, in its bulk with the mighty overhang soaring into the air, a challenge for the impalpable matter of the sea it encounters.

Already in the 60s the forward-looking Marshall McLuhan had asserted that our clothes and houses are the extension of our skin. The digital has turned our skin, which in Venturian research was mimetic and citationist, into media clothing.

A *Kunsthalle* could not be interpreted better than by a pair of artists who had always been involved in the ungraspable dimension of art. They consider their architecture to be composed of layers and their desire is to have the public penetrate into its innermost substance.

As Liz Diller states, the museum is composed of two parts, the public building realized from the ground upwards, the intimate one from the sky downwards. The space has been thought of as a public walkway which winds towards a stairway-grandstand from

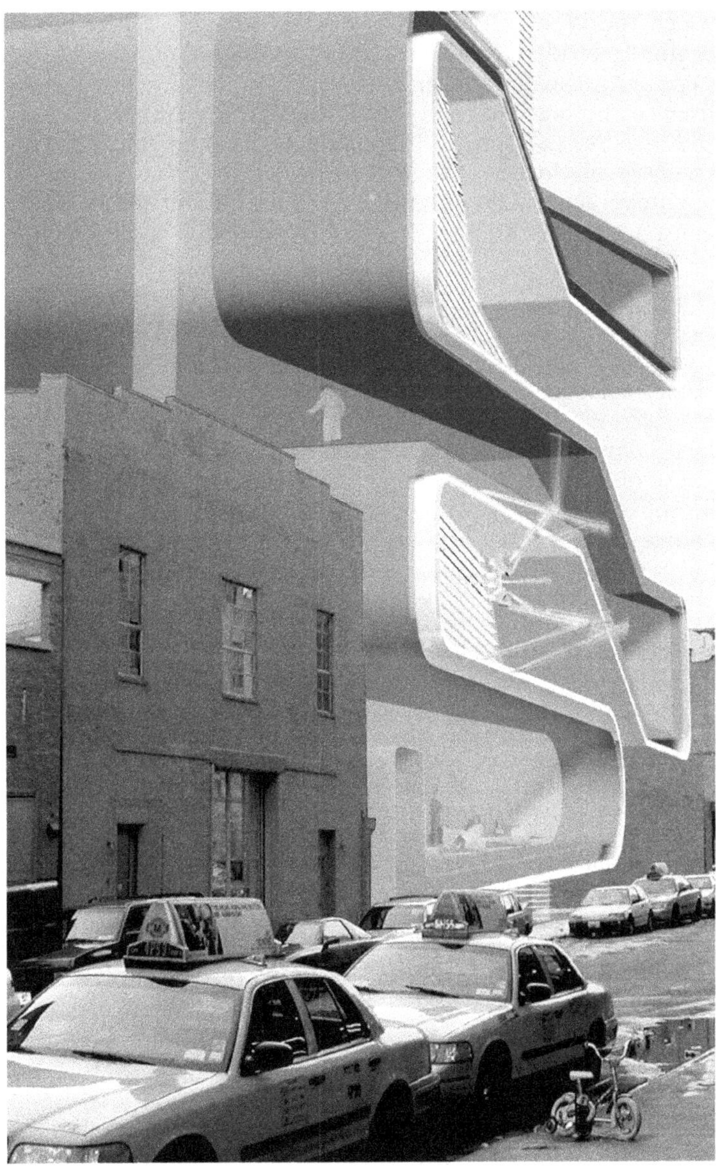

EYEBEAM MUSEUM OF ART & TECHNOLOGY, *NEW YORK, 2007*

which the view of the harbor can be enjoyed. The stairway continues inside the building and in cross-section becomes the steps of the theater, to then curve round in the direction it came from and become the gallery level. This is situated in the overhang and is a dramatic spread. The material enveloping the gallery is highly technological: steel and lenticular glass that changes in brightness depending on the observer's position, making the space indistinct.

> The north face of the Long Gallery that connects east and west galleries is made of lenticular glass. Composed of microscopic vertical lenses that permit vision out when viewed in the perpendicular direction but arrest vision when viewed on the oblique, the view opens up as one passes, producing the uncanny effect for the viewer of being "followed" by the view (D + S 2004).

D + S develop the sensory experiment linked with sight and the denial of sight. The media library level, where the Internet access is, slopes at an angle of 30°, with an opening to create a floor entirely in glass that juts out framing the water. In Boston they have revisited the theme of transparency and the social implications linked with it.

> The Modernist project is still largely unfinished and that leaves us room to reinterpret. The democratizing aspirations of curtain wall technology and unfettered vision, for example, led to the realization that glass was a two-way system which several decades later bred the desire for privacy and mirrored glass. However, yesterday's fear of being watched has turned into today's fear that no one is watching. There has never been such an obsession with transparency. The lightening of curtain wall detailing has reached unprecedented levels of virtuosity. What was once a medium to look through is now a medium to look at. Buildings and their occupants have become equal exhibitionists (D + S 2004).

Thanks to the new electronic technologies, the glass the museum structure is made of can appear translucent or completely opaque depending on the theatrical or display requirements. At night the gallery is illuminated, turning the museum into a radiant new symbol for the city of Boston. While the stairway leads to the theater, the entrance is situated at ground level. This ritual aspect of the ascent, which D + S often develop in their projects, aims at a sort of questioning of the system of expectation and conventional functioning of Neoclassical and eclectic museums, with their customs motivated by strong class division. Reflecting on the public climbing then descending again is almost a game, a Dada invention, a paradox by the irreverent pair. The new museum stands as a work of art and not an acritical container, following the lesson instigated by Wright and acknowledged by Gehry and Libeskind.

5.5 Ribbon or interface

In 2003 the Whitney Museum of New York dedicated an important retrospective exhibition to Diller & Scofidio's work of over twenty years. The two architects opted for an evocative display and retrieved from the Museum of Modern Art (NYC) the wall where for years Marcel Duchamp's famous work *Standard Stoppages* had been placed, stripping off the plaster, as occurs for archaeological frescoes, and placing it in a hall at the Whitney.
Among the various works exhibited the *Eyebeam Atelier of New* **68-69**
Media & Technology project stood out, located in Chelsea, the historic district of New York hosting important art galleries. The museum plan is a curved ribbon which, as it develops, generates spatiality in the absence of obstacles. In 1858 August Ferdinand Möbius constructed the famous ring that took his name. Digital architecture has interpreted the extraordinary intuition of this famous German mathematician and astronomer. In 1998 the UN Studio van Berkel & Bos realized the *Möbius House*. Since then a whole generation of architects have made the philosophy of the ribbon their own, in which internal and external, dream and reality interrelate. The theme of the sensitive surface, of space folding round itself in a continuous route is central to today's experiments with the digital, to the extent that the French philosopher Pierre Lévy coined the term "Möbius effect".

When the competition for the *Eyebeam* was announced the most innovative groups on the digital scene took part, including MVRDV, Asymptote, FOA, Greg Lynn FORM, Reiser + Umemoto. Among the proposals that of Hani Rashid and Lise Anne Couture of Asymptote appeared as a modeled, sculpted structure. The museum as a complex box was experienced via ramps and spirals, within the virtual world. The winning proposal by D + S was undoubtedly the most innovative. The pair eliminated the box and translated the project into an articulate

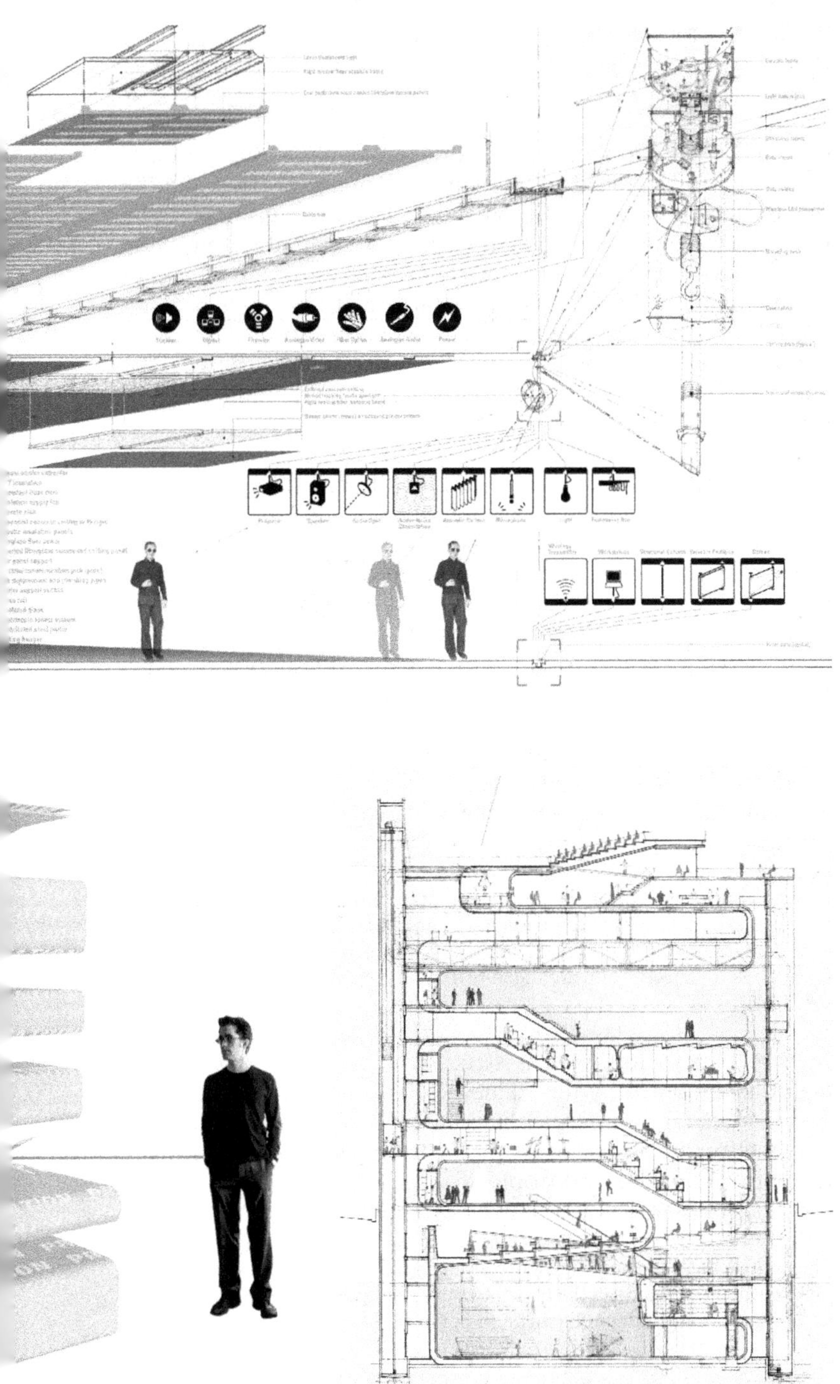

system of links: a ribbon as an interface, like a net to receive and transmit information. The museum is an image of itself and the functions contained in it. In contrast with the Möbius philosophy the ribbon does not end. In their view an unqualifiable dimension of something unresolved is always present. The ribbon cannot join up again or generate a temporal circuit that folds back on itself. D + S claimed, like in Beckett's famous novel *Waiting for Godot,* a waiting period, a ribbon that possessed the energy to be able to grow further. This project belonged to the dimension of spirals.
In 1961, at the Los Angeles Museum of Science and Industry, Charles and Ray Eames took care of the scenography for the exhibition *Mathematica, a world of numbers and beyond*, where the Möbius circular sculpture condensed their research on form. There is always a sort of inexplicable magic that binds designers who work as a pair. The Eames', architects, designers, graphics and communicators had already interpreted the project in the 60s as "the art of solving problems by setting up relations". They translated every idea into a project, convinced that all things are architecture, thus breaking down the hard and fast limits of the functionalist programs. They worked on the relations between society and technology, certain that delimited, enclosed pertinent areas did not exist, but everything could converge in the creative process.

> If you consider a broader definition of technology you realize that architecture is already a product of political, economic, and social technologies. Material and electronic technologies add more to the palette. Bricks, bits, and pixels form architecture's irreducible units of construction (D + S 2004).

In D + S' museum what is striking is the translation of the materials modeled by the Eames' into an architectural project. The new digital technologies have enabled the transfer of insights deriving from the world of art, mathematics and design, allowing – through a spatial, philosophical and technical revolution – obstacles of a structural type to be overcome.

72-73 The spatial logic of the proposed building is based on a simple premise: a pliable ribbon that locates the two major program pieces, *production* [atelier] and *presentation* [museum/theater] on opposing faces. The ribbon undulates from side to side as it climbs vertically from the street, floor folding into wall, folding into floor, folding into wall... With each change of direction, the ribbon alternately enfolds a production space or a presentation space (D + S 2004).

The choice is to create a continuous space using a ribbon that folds as it rises vertically, to reach 12 floors. The cement and steel framework, developed as a multi-directional surface, would contain all the plant inside it. The interstitial gap between the two folds would host the building's nervous system.
D + S are used to working on themes; their experience in the performance sphere has led them to thoroughly examine the difficulties present in the field of action. The museum for the new media and technologies could not be imagined as a box-building, but suited to the new electronic paradigms (interactivity, fluidity, information), like an installation made of places which alternate in a sequence so as to determine a genetic code.
The lightness and speed Calvino prophetically foresees in *Lezioni Americane* are vigorously stated in this project. While the UN Studio's *Mercedes Benz Museum* in Stuttgart was invented as a spiral, generated by an ascending double helix, like a continuous pathway that makes the observer constantly change position, the Eyebeam espouses structural dynamism and incomplete closure of the ribbon. It appears with fascinating spatiality at ground level enabling the whole of the museum to be visualized. The computerized sequence 0 1 is the genesis of the museum activities that reproduce the same division. The diagonal development of the framework takes its distance once and for all from Modernist linear logic. Everything is in the light of day, there are no areas that cannot be visited; the museum represents the new frontier of the net, accessible and connected. The challenge D + S propose with information architecture interfacing with the exterior is one of the themes introduced. Let us see the possible developments.
In a brief essay entitled *From the other side of the telescope*, when speaking of interfaces, Derrick de Kerckhove suggests the hypothesis of new possible developments of connective architecture: "Yesterday: paper and pen – today: vocal commands – tomorrow: direct link mind/machine. [...] Will we connect with the environment with the same intimacy with which we are linked with our body?" (De Kerckhove 98).
If we look at the latest research by Marcos Novak (*Echinoderm*)

LINCOLN CENTER FOR THE PERFORMING ARTS, *NEW YORK, 2008*

The project to restore the Lincoln Center aims at giving back life to the famous New York district by using I.T. systems. The Studio reconsiders spaces carrying out painless restoration, into which technology is fitted to give new transparency. The North Plaza is studied as a new public context, but the interventions diversify in restoring the facade, to the point of acoustic remodulation of the Alice Tully Hall.

On the opposite page:
SLITHER BUILDING, *GIFU, JAPAN, 2000*

This is a residential intervention that fits into the masterplan designed by Isozaki. The building highlights the limits of standardization and seeks possible variations on this theme. The body is treated as a transparent skin and brings to mind the scenarios investigated several years earlier by the Morphosis.

and Kas Oosterhuis (*Trans-ports*), still at an experimental level, scenarios that could be realized in the future are materializing.
The area in which the museum was to be built shows brick buildings of the early 1900s in New York, and is proud of the strong attitude of the new intervention. Together with dBox, D + S made the video *16 hours*, invented as an actual film based on the techniques of virtual animation, which allowed the functioning, the bold perspectives and various programs to be seen in real time, anticipating actual realization of the project.

> The alternating programs also comb together two diverse populations: the building's residents [students, artists and staff] and the building's visitors [museum and theater-goers]. Each population passes by or through the spaces of the other while moving between successive levels. The interface between these two groups becomes more intricate where a fold of ribbon shears and partially slips into alignment with a level above or below, allowing a production space to infiltrate an exhibition level or vice versa. This *controlled contamination* juxtaposes spaces of diverse qualities, activities and speed (D + S 2004).

When the flows of the different populations overlap, the video shows the different observation points that clarify both the museum spaces and its flexible functioning, and the possibility of originating casual encounters. The animated video greatly contributed to clarifying the project amid the artistic installations, interactive screens and sensitive environments. The "virtual" has the strength to foresee the museum spaces, generating places that can be passed through and visited, that are tangible.

5.6 Interactive landscape

The first Universal Exposition, held London in 1851, marked a deep-seated revolution in architecture both in the structural field and the perceptive one with the creation of *Crystal Palace*. Architecture just of iron and glass, in a classical framework, carried out by the greenhouse constructor Joseph Paxton. Opening up this route brought many apparent contradictions, almost a point of no return. This work expressed the culture of the early era of machinery. More than a century later, Eero Saarinen and Charles Eames realized a masterpiece at the New York World Fair (1964-65): a theater supported by a forest of masts of Corten

steel, enclosed in an ovoid. A suspended, enclosed theater, a classical theme and an innovative solution.
In 2002 for the Swiss Expo the D + S company were invited to design the temporary exhibition pavilion *Blur* on Neuchâtel Lake at Yverdon-les-Bains. 80-81

> The new challenge for us was the responsibility of appealing to a mass audience. Prior to this, our audience was limited to educated, high-cultured, progressively-minded, metropolitan people. Our work unwittingly targeted this distinct subculture of which we were members. The *Blur Building* on the other hand had to work for every age group and economic and social strata. We accomplished this by defying expectations. People visiting world expositions expect to see displays of nationalism and technological progress. In any case they expect to *see*. We decidedly wanted to make a building which problematized seeing ... a building in which there was nothing to see and nothing to do. It was a building about nothing, but spectacularly about nothing (D + S 2004).

At Yverdon they combined two distinct utopias, incongruous like the times they had been investigating for years. For the steel structure recalls the experiment begun in the 40s/50s by Buckminster Fuller on structures embracing empty spaces inside. The architects realized a platform based on the construction of an ellipse, with notable dimensions – 100 m x 60 m x 10 m – placed 15 m from the level of the lake. The pavilion was a steel *tensegrity* structure with bipyramidal cells supported by 4 columns.
The theme 'I and the universe', on which the designers were called to give a solution, clarified the intent of the project: the circular form recalled Renaissance studies that considered the universe a finished, circular form as in the Neoplatonic tradition of circles. The structure appears as enigmatic, detached from the ground, calling to mind Kiesler's work, who incredibly constructed enveloping structures that were detached from the ground. At Yverdon, too, D + S detached the building from the water level like a structure on stilts, well-soldered on four robust pylons.
What, then, was innovative about this project that had such amazing fortune?
When the machine is turned off it is silent. This project was the American Studio's obsession for two years. They decided to make the pavilion-structure disappear in a cloud of steam that was visible at a distance by the Expo visitor. Hence the large structure is run by a computer that operates 31,500 nozzles which take water

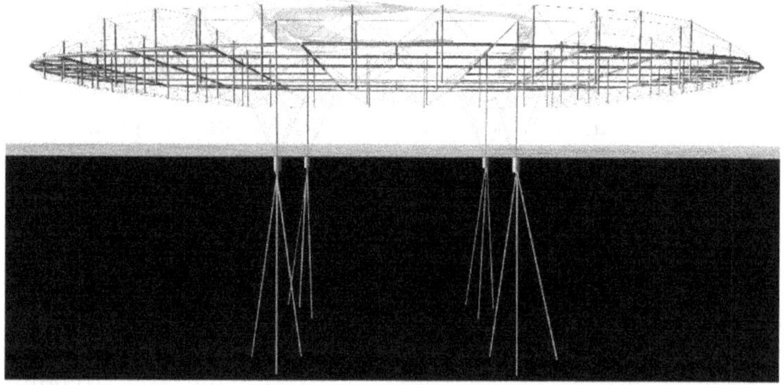

BLUR BUILDING, *LAKE NEUCHATEL, YVERDON-LES-BAINS, SWITZERLAND, 2002*

up from the lake and nebulize it at great pressure. D + S go to the extreme limits with their research on the digital. The connected machine thus translates into an intelligent, disturbing system that takes life from the actual substance it rests on. Water is the new element that the digital investigates. The ways of interpreting this are varied, but all address the visitor's psychological and sensory perception. The virtual and the digital have introduced a new dimension that involves and modifies the system of expectation and creates surprise. An interactive work of art that makes the stable substance of the lake pulsate with an indefinite blurring causing the borders of reality to be lost. In *Blur* they seek physical and emotional interaction with the visitor.

"Physical interactivity means that the architecture itself changes, enabling the change in situations and desires to be expressed. [...] The fact is that architecture may react, but may also inter-react, namely adapt itself to the change in desires of the users by scenarios that can be experienced like a hypertext" (Saggio 2003). The experience translates from visual to sensorial when the visitor passes through a double walkway in fiberglass 100 meters long onto the floating platform. The nebulized cloud makes perception indistinct and blurred. Technology is never a neutral system and the water moistens the intelligent raincoats equipped with sensors that become colored or emit sounds based on particular stimulation. For D + S atmospheric weather converts into a global theme, universally comprehensible. In the relationship between individuality and the infinite they introduce an indescribable, immeasurable dimension, giving the climate and the winds the chance to change the mass, the consistency and the actual nature
84-85 of their invention.

From the 80s onwards Toyo Ito and Jean Nouvel were the architects who opened the way to dematerialized architecture. In 1999 Ito theorized on *Blurring Architecture* in an exhibition held in Aachen and subsequently in Tokyo. Ito pointed out that: "*Blur* means to make misty, fade or be indistinct, unclear. Thus *Blurring Architecture* takes on the meaning of "architecture with imprecise limits". It refers to architecture with oscillating, sinuous limits that look like those of objects in a lake with rough water" (Ito 99).

This indistinct, unclear, blurred state recalls the turbulence created when the waters of two rivers mix as they converge, and it brings to mind Leonardo's studies on water flows.

In 2003 Eisenman published the text *Blurred Zones. Investigations of the interstitial* where he handled the theme of *blurring*. In an interview with Günther Uhlig the architect clarified his view: "*Blurring* is the attempt to deny the original value, the metaphysics of the presence, the motivation of signs and the desire for information" (Eisenman 2000).
If the culture of the 80s had introduced the demolition of material structures and in the 90s algorithms showed us new form-generating structures, at Yverdon D + S shift the attention to a structure that disappears, loses significance, represents the non-definable and clarifies a new route, perhaps never again practicable between form and representation. The intelligent machine is the new challenge of the electronic era; it shows a new interpretation that breaks away from a clear vision (the term "perspective", from *perspectiva,* means "see distinctly, with clarity") in favor of a non-definite one that has deeply touched the visitors' soul, as was the intention of the designers. Digital technology, having at last acquired knowledge of a structural nature, opens its gaze towards the indistinct, the unmeasurable, a different gaze out of the window, to arouse emotions. The space of the modern body, depicted by the mechanism metaphor, is transformed into the electronic body. D + S thus intend to challenge the principles that have always configured the architecture discipline, founded on the definition of dialectical pairs (inside/outside, closed/open). *Blur* literally means out of focus and describes a non-distinguishable dimension. Concepts like near/far, internal/external lose their meaning. They realize their most complex work by upsetting that which throughout the history of man defined his capacity to survive: the sense of sight. Once the visitor has entered the *Blur*, s/he experiences a sense of disorientation, due to a change in perception; there is nothing to see, except our dependence on sight itself.

We also twisted and applied knowledge from the theater, re-engineering attention span and redefining spectacle. Our own mandate was to make a spectacle that was not dependent on a theatrical arc. Unlike the focused spectacle normally conceived for a collected audience, we wanted to make a diffuse spectacle for a wandering audience that stretched attention span through an attenuated sense of discomfort (D + S 2004).

In 1990 Jacques Derrida wrote *Memoirs of the Blind* in which he investigated the theme of blindness in the history of painting. He deconstructed the idea of clear, distinct vision in favor of a memory of the image in which the visible conceals the invisible or the not yet seen. In his conception the image is no longer the point of arrival so much as the threshold beyond which to see, which at the same time shows its blind point. Derrida explains that vision can no longer be satisfied by sight alone, but needs to be transferred to the other senses. "Hearing goes farther than the hand, which goes farther than the eye" (Derrida 2003).

The indefinite and the inexplicable have belonged to the artistic and literary dimension and have passed through history over the centuries. In *The unknown masterpiece,* written in 1832 and set in the Paris of 1600, Honoré de Balzac reflects on the true essence of art. The very young Nicolas Poussin visits the studio of the painter Francis Porbus. As destiny would have it, here he meets Frenhofer the elderly, brusque painter, holder of the "secret of painting", who has been working for ten years in total isolation and secrecy on his masterpiece, the *Belle Noiseuse*. The artist seeks absolute beauty in this work. To complete his painting he needs a model who will embody this ideal. With great difficulty Poussin convinces his Gillette to pose. Having won over Frenhofer's resistance to show the completed work, Porbus and Poussin discover that the mysterious masterpiece is actually a mass of "colors thrown together in a muddle running in a thousand strange rivulets and forming a wall of paint". From this shapeless matter appears a woman's foot, perfectly painted. Balzac anticipates a focal point of the research that would strike the 1900s, the shift of art towards the shapeless, indescribable world that is fleeting, no longer in focus.

At Yverdon, Diller and Scofidio, always interested in the use of high definition technology as a medium, interpret the site as a sheet and use the water to disconcert sight, to produce – as the designers themselves assert – anti-heroic architecture, low definition technology, indistinct like a cloud, through the best developed system that technology makes available, so as to amplify the atmosphere of uncertainty caused by the mist. The blurring is also a mechanism of defense from surveillance. Here technology is used against itself. Matter, space and information enter into the virtual dimension. The formal has dissolved in the sentient. And the landscape, becoming liquid, has acquired an autonomous, disturbing life, palpitating and pulsating.

When Papini wrote the book *GOG* in 1931, when the Futurist mood was at its height, he dedicated a tale to the new sculpture, with a mixture of irony, fun and new consciousness. "Come, he said to me. You'll see what you'll not be able to see in any gallery or exhibition in the world. After thousands of years I've inaugurated a new kind of sculpture, never done by anyone before. [...] Didn't I tell you I've learnt to create the 'never seen'.

I am a sculptor too! – but not in the usual unrefined way. The ancient massive, heavy sculpture inherited from the Egyptians and the Assyrians has had its time. It corresponded to religious, monarchical, slow, primitive civilizations. Nowadays we are skeptical, anarchical, dynamic, cinematic. [...] The only plastic solution possible consists of passing from immobility to ephemerality". Thus the sculptor began working with his hands on the sculpture of smoke. "Look at it! Quickly! Lock up the form in your memory! In a few seconds the statue will vanish like a dying melody! [...] – The masterpiece is dead just as all masterpieces die! What does it matter! I can make it again, as many as I like! Each work is unique and has to suffice for the joy of a single minute. If a statue lasts ten centuries or ten seconds what difference is there compared with eternity, for be it of marble or smoke it will disappear in the end".

At Yverdon-les-bains D + S switch on the sensitive machine, release the cloud of dew on the sentient public, reconstruct a blurred image of the lake that for thousands of years has remained unchanged, and on the theme 'I and the universe' choose a rapid emotion that dissolves.

For further study

The main texts used in this book belong to the literary criticism of Diller + Scofidio, together with the philosophical theories expressed principally by Foucault, Deleuze, Derrida and Baudrillard up to the most recent ones that investigate the relation between architecture and information in the theoretical works of Virilio, De Kerckhove and Saggio. These contributions intertwine directly and crosswise with the works of the American Studio. This has enabled me to weave relations at a distance with D + S' production, endowed with many levels of reading, with the purpose of making the deepest layers emerge.

Baudrillard 96 - Jean Baudrillard, *Il delitto perfetto. La televisione ha ucciso la realtà?*, Raffaello Cortina Editore, Milan 1996.

Betsky 2003 - Aaron Betsky, *The aberrant architectures of Diller + Scofidio*, Whitney Museum of American Art, Harry N. Abrams, New York 2003.

D + S 94a - Diller + Scofidio, *Back to the front: Tourisms of war / Visite aux armées: tourismes de guerre*, F.R.A.C., Basse-Normandie 1994.

D + S 94b - Diller + Scofidio, *Flesh. Architectural probes*, Princeton Architectural Press, New York 1994.

D + S 2002 - Diller + Scofidio, *Blur: the making of nothing*, Harry N. Abrams, New York 2002.

D + S 2004 - The quotations on Diller + Scofidio's ideas are part of a long interview granted to the author by the architects for this book and translated for the Italian version by Barbara Pasqualetto.

De Kerckhove 98 - Derrick de Kerckhove, *Dall'altro lato del telescopio*, in «Domus», n. 800, January 1998.

Derrida 2003 - Jacques Derrida, *Memorie di cieco. L'autoritratto e altre rovine*, Abscondita, Milan 2003.

Eisenman 2000 - Peter Eisenman speaking to Günter Uhlig, *Il carattere critico dell'architettura*, in «Domus», n. 824, March 2000.

Foucault 76 - Michel Foucault, *Sorvegliare e punire. Nascita della prigione*, Einaudi, Turin 1976.

Hejduk 84 - John Hejduk, *Kinney House. Un progetto di Ricardo Scofidio e Elizabeth Diller*, in «Lotus International», n. 44, 1984.

Ito 99 - Toyo Ito, *Blurring Architecture* [1999], in Giovanni Longobardi, *Toyo Ito. Antologia di testi su L'architettura evanescente*, Edizioni Kappa, Rome 2003.

Lyon 97 - David Lyon, *L'occhio elettronico. Privacy e filosofia della sorveglianza*, Feltrinelli, Milan 1997.

McLuhan 64 - Marshall McLuhan, *Understanding Media: The Extensions of Man*, Routledge and Kegan Paul, London 1964.

Pongratz - Perbellini 2000 - Christian Pongratz, Maria Rita Perbellini, *Nati con il computer. Giovani architetti americani*, Testo & Immagine, Turin 2000.

Ragon 74 - Michel Ragon, *Storia dell'architettura e dell'urbanistica moderne*, Editori Riuniti, Rome 1974.

Saggio 2000 - Antonino Saggio, *Nuove sostanze. L'informatica e il rinnovamento dell'architettura*, in «Il Progetto», n. 6, January 2000.

Saggio 2003 - Antonino Saggio, *L'architettura informa*, in Furio Barzon, *La carta*

di Zurigo. Eisenman, De Kerckhove, Saggio, Testo & Immagine, Turin 2003.
Teyssot 90 - Georges Teyssot, *Cancellazione e scorporamento. Dialoghi con Diller + Scofidio*, in «Ottagono», n. 96, September 1990.
Virilio 2000 - Paul Virilio, *Dal Media Building alla città globale*, in «Crossing», n. 1, December 2000.
Wigley 90 - Mark Wigley, *La disciplina dell'architettura*, in «Ottagono», n. 96, September 1990.

1. The 70s, the Apple rebels

1.1 Outside the system
On teaching architecture at American universities see Issue 27 of «Lotus International» [1980]. In particular the profiles of Cornell, Cooper Union and Columbia are outlined. For further study I suggest: *Education of an Architect: a point of view*. The book was presented on the occasion of the Cooper Union exhibition at MoMA, New York 1971, and exhibits the work of students in connection with Hejduk's teaching method.
For a picture of the cultural transformations D + S interpret from the cinema, theater and philosophy see Teyssot 90, pp. 56–89.

1.2 The body without organs
The relation existing between body and architecture changes through the centuries, from the Vitruvian studies to today's theories on the bachelor machine and the recent conceptions of artificial man.
The text that challenges psychoanalytic theories, analysing the body as a constantly rewriteable surface, is Deleuze and Guattari's *L'Anti-Edipo. Capitalismo e schizofrenia* (Einaudi) [1972]. The philosophers study the formation of the oedipal structure from primitive society to capitalism. Schizophrenia translates as the limit of capitalism, in which the subject is freed from social conventions. In the text they introduce the theme of desiring machines, shifting the attention to desire against the need that had marked Freudian theories and Modernity. On these issues D + S were to be an interface with multimedia and theater works like *Jet Lag* and *Moving Target*.
In the 90s Teyssot dedicated a series of important essays to clarifying the new frontiers both in the field of art and that of philosophy. I suggest: Teyssot 90, p. 72; Georges Teyssot, *The mutant body of architecture* in D + S 94b, pp. 8–35; Georges Teyssot, *Body-Building. Verso un nuovo organicismo*, in «Lotus International», n. 94, 1997, pp. 118–131.
On the new subjectivity see Antonino Saggio's work: Saggio 2000, pp. 32-35; Saggio 2003, pp. 73-87.

2. New rites

2.1 Prosthetic Theory
There is a vast body of literature on the topic, both cinematographic, from Ridley Scott to David Cronenberg, and literary, including the visionary, apocalyptic production of Philip K. Dick (*Ma gli androidi sognano pecore*

elettroniche? [1968], Fanucci Editore, Rome 2000; *I labirinti della memoria*, Fanucci Editore, Rome 2004), as well as theoretical, in the writings of Donna Haraway, of which *A Manifesto for Cyborgs: Science, Technology, and Socialist Feminism in the 1980s* remains a reference point (published in 1985 by «Socialist Review» and in 1995 by Feltrinelli). I suggest some writings tackling the theme of prosthetic architecture that were published in the thematic issue of «Ottagono» n. 96 (September 1990): Wigley 90, pp. 19–27; Anthony Vidler, *Case per cyborg. Protesi domestiche da Salvador Dalì a Diller e Scofidio*, pp. 36–55; Jacques Guillerme, *Tesi sulla protesi: il pretesto dei bisogni latenti*, pp. 105–113.

2.2 The bachelor machine

Elizabeth Diller & Ricardo Scofidio, *A delay in glass. Performance architettonica di un'opera di Duchamp*, in «Lotus International», n. 53, 1987, pp. 22-31.

On Marcel Duchamp's complex work *La mariée mise à nu par ses célibataires* see Guido Ballo, *Occhio critico 2. La chiave dell'arte moderna*, Longanesi, Milan 1968, p. 286.

For in-depth study of the Dada movement: Various Authors, *Dada. L'arte della negazione*, Edizione De Luca, Rome 1994.

2.3 Travel and new territories

On the theme of tourism see the chapter *Turismo e viaggio, paesaggio e scrittura* by Marc Augé in *Rovine e Macerie. Il senso del tempo*, Bollati Boringhieri, Turin 2004, pp. 49-79. On the same topic: D + S 94a; D + S 94b, pp. 198–220.

2.4 The sensitive fold

The installation *Bad Press* was presented in 1998 at the 6th International Architecture Exhibition in Venice and respective catalogue *Sensori del futuro. L'architetto come sismografo*, Electa, Venice 1996, pp. 184–185.

On the installation: Erwin J. S. Viray, *Fashionable collaborations*, in A + U: «Architecture and Urbanism», n. 12 (375), December 2001, pp. 78–81.

The theme of the fold is central to digital studies; I suggest some fundamental texts: Gilles Deleuze, *La piega. Leibniz e il barocco*, Einaudi, Turin 1990; Greg Lynn, *Folding in Architecture*, Architectural Design, Academy Editions, London 1993; Bernard Cache, *Earth Moves: The Furnishing of Territories*, The MIT Press, Cambridge, Mass. 1995.

See also: Georges Teyssot, *Soglie e pieghe. Sull'intérieur e l'interiorità*, in «Casabella», n. 681, September 2000, pp. 26–35; Alicia Imperiale, *Nuove Bidimensionalità. Tensioni superficiali nell'architettura digitale*, Testo & Immagine, Turin 2001; Antonello Marotta, *Ben van Berkel. La prospettiva rovesciata di UN Studio*, Testo & Immagine, Turin 2003.

3. Between inside and outside

3.1 The non-signifying window-module

Andrew Bartle and Jonathan Kirschenfeld published an interesting essay on recent architecture in the eastern United States in «Ottagono» n. 86 (1987)

entitled *L'analogo e l'anomalo. Architettura e quotidiano*, useful for interpreting the cultural phenomena from which Diller and Scofidio partly descend (pp. 20–23).
A fundamental article was written on *Kinney House* by John Hejduk, a friend and teacher of Diller and admirer of their work: Hejduk 84, pp. 58–63.
On Duchamp's work *Porta: rue Larrey* see Georges Teyssot, *Paesaggi d'interni / Interior Landscapes*, in «Quaderni di Lotus», n. 8, Electa 1987, p. 72. In the same review, regarding the window theme: Elizabeth Diller and Ricardo Scofidio, *Inside-out: la finestra sul giardino*, pp. 66–69.

3.2 The virtual house
The Slow House is included in the catalogue edited by Terence Riley, *The Un-Private House*, The Museum of Modern Art, New York 1999.
Alex Bremner, *Re-activating the docile body: a critical (re)view of Diller + Scofidio's "Slow House"*, in «Architectural Theory Review», vol. 5 n. 1, April 2000, pp. 104-122.

4. The worlds of reflection

4.1 Nijinski's diaries
On the theater – architecture theme see Fulvio Irace, *Scenografia, architettura e allestimento teatrale*, pp. 123–124, and Michele Porcu, *Danzare di architettura: Frédéric Flamand*, pp. 126–127, in «Abitare», n. 401, December 2000.
On the spatial transformations in the theater of the 20s in Vienna and the innovative work of Frederick Kiesler in connection with scenic space: Maria Bottero, *Frederick Kiesler. Arte, Architettura, Ambiente*, Milan Triennial, Electa, Milan 1995, pp. 20–23 (*La matrice simbolica del teatro, ovvero l'architettura d'azione*), pp. 38–42 (*Il teatro come invenzione totale*), pp. 49–53 (*Vienna e l'Europa 1923–1925*).
Regarding Gropius' *Total Theater*: Christian Norberg-Schulz, *Bauhaus*, Officina Edizioni, Rome 1986, pp. 24–25.
Artaud's theater was explored by Jacques Derrida in *La scrittura e la differenza*, Biblioteca Einaudi, Turin 1971, in the chapters: *Artaud: la parola soufflée*, pp. 219–254, and *Il teatro della crudeltà e la chiusura della rappresentazione*, pp. 299–323.

4.2 Deferred time
On *Cyberspace*: William Gibson, *Neuromante*, Editrice Nord, Milan 1986.
For an introduction to the themes investigating the media and social repercussions see: Paul Virilio, *The Third Window: an interview with Paul Virilio*, in Cynthia Schneider and Brian Wallis, *Global Television*, Wedge Press, New York 1988; Gianni Vattimo, *La società trasparente*, Garzanti, Milan 1989; Baudrillard 96; Jacques Derrida, Bernard Stiegler, *Ecografie della televisione*, Raffaello Cortina Editore, Milan 1997; Pierre Lévy, *L'intelligenza collettiva. Per una antropologia del cyberspazio* [1994], Feltrinelli, Milan 2002.
Christian Pongratz and Maria Rita Perbellini analysed telematic architecture in Diller and Scofidio's work in Pongratz - Perbellini 2000, pp. 60–66.

5. Connective architecture

5.1 The society of control
George Orwell, *1984*, Oscar Mondadori, Milan 1973, (published in 1949).
On the "control" and society theme: Foucault 76; Lyon 97.
See also *Prigioni / Programmi di controllo elettronico* in William J. Mitchell, *La città dei bits. Spazi, luoghi e autostrade informatiche*, Electa, Milan 1997, p. 44.

5.2 Screens and displays
In the 60s Marshall McLuhan, philosopher and sociologist, was the greatest theorist of the new media, see: Marshall McLuhan, *Gli strumenti del comunicare*, Il Saggiatore, Milan 1967; Marshall McLuhan, *La legge dei media: la nuova scienza*, Edizioni Lavoro, Rome 1994.
I also suggest the essays: Paul Virilio, *Lo spazio critico*, Edizioni Dedalo, Bari 1998; Derrick de Kerckhove, *L'architettura dell'intelligenza*, Testo & Immagine, Turin 2001; Giampiero Bosoni, *La pelle tatuata dell'architettura contemporanea: storia dell'architettura a funzione multimediale*, in «Crossing», n. 1, December 2000, pp. 72-81.
On the *Media Building*: Virilio 2000, pp. 5–11.
On the installation *Cold War*: Diller and Scofidio, *Permanent installation sunrise*, in «Casabella», n. 673/674 (*USA, architettura come spettacolo*), December 1999 – January 2000, pp. 101–103.
Regarding the installation *Facsimile*: «Casabella», n. 673/674, pp. 104–105; Edward Dimendberg, *L'architettura rovesciata: soglie urbane e immagine digitale*, in *Metamorph. 9th International Architecture Exhibition*, Venice Biennial, Marsilio, Venice 2004, pp. 82–93.
On *Travelogues*: Catherine Slessor, *Life in limbo*, in «The Architectural Review», vol. 212 n. 1269, November 2002, pp. 30–31.

5.3 Lunch with Mies
Guy Debord, *La società dello spettacolo* [1967], Baldini & Castoldi, Milan 1997.
Art as spectacle: Pat Hackett (edited by), *I diari di Andy Warhol*, De Agostini, Novara 1989.
On the *Brasserie*: Nicola Turner, *Gin Palace*, in «World Architecture», n. 88, July/August 2000, pp. 86–91; Jan Abrams, *Il ristorante come spettacolo*, in «Domus», n. 830, October 2000, pp. 118–125; Philip Jodidio, *Architecture Now!*, Taschen, Cologne 2001, (*Brasserie*, pp. 162–167); Claudia Banz, *Brasserie in New York*, in «Detail», vol. 41 n. 2, March 2001, pp. 236–241; Diller and Scofidio, *The Brasserie, The Seagram Building, New York, USA 2000*, in A + U: «Architecture and Urbanism», n. 368, May 2001, pp. 70–77; Catherine Slessor, *Open and shut case*, in «World Architecture», n. 104, March 2002, pp. 62–64.

5.4 Digital waterfront
On the *ICA* project: Alan G. Brake, *Diller + Scofidio: Institute of Contemporary Art*, Boston, Mass., in «Architecture», vol. 91 n. 10, October 2002, pp. 30–31; Daniel Herman, *Room with a view*, in «Artforum International», vol. 41 n. 3, November 2002, p. 56.
On the theme of the skin as media dress: Toyo Ito, *L'immagine dell'architettura*

nell'era dell'elettronica, in «Domus», n. 800, January 1998, pp. 28–29.

5.5 Ribbon or interface
On the retrospective exhibition at the Whitney: Sharon McHugh, *Diller + Scofidio: New York – Boston*, in «Abitare», n. 426, March 2003, pp. 43–44; Suzane Wines, *Architettura inaspettata / Unexpected architecture: the aberrant architectures of Diller + Scofidio*, in «Domus», n. 858, April 2003, pp. 27–29; John E. Czarnecki, *Diller + Scofidio challenge assumptions in the first major American exhibition*, in «Architectural Record», vol. 191 n. 4, April 2003, pp. 103–104.
On the *Eyebeam Atelier*: Diller + Scofidio, *Eyebeam School, New York*, in *Next. 8th International Architecture Exhibition*, Marsilio, Venice 2002, pp.160–163; Catherine Slessor, *Creative interaction*, in «The Architectural Review», vol. 212 n. 1269, November 2002, pp. 76–77; Diller + Scofidio, *Eyebeam Museum of Art and Technology*, in «Architecture», vol. 92 n. 1, January 2003, pp. 76–77; Philip Jodidio, *Architecture Now! vol. 2*, Taschen, Cologne 2003, (*Eyebeam Institute*, pp. 142–147).

5.6 Interactive landscape
On interactivity: Antonino Saggio, *Nuova soggettività. L'architettura tra comunicazione e informazione*, in «Op. Cit.», n. 112, 2001, pp. 14-21; Antonino Saggio, *Interactivity at the Centre of Avant-Garde Architectural Research*, in «Architectural Design», vol. 75 n. 1, January 2005, pp. 23-29.
On *Blurring Architecture*: Ito 99, p. 94; Toyo Ito, *Blurring Architecture*, Charta, Milan 2000; Eisenman 2000, pp. 4–8; *Blurred zones. Investigations of the Interstitial, Eisenman Architects 1988–1998*, The Monacelli Press, 2003; Paola Gregory, *Territori della complessità. New Scapes*, Testo & Immagine, Turin 2003, pp. 88–89.
On the *Blur Building*: *PA [Progressive Architecture] Awards 2000*, in «Architecture», vol. 89 n. 4, April 2000, pp. 90–95; Philip Jodidio, *Architecture Now!*, Taschen, Cologne 2001, (*Blur Building*, pp. 168–173); Kieran Long, *Lake eerie: Expo 2002, Switzerland*, in «World Architecture», n. 107, June 2002, pp. 40–48; *Expo 02: exposition nationale suisse*, in «Techniques & Architecture», n. 460, June/July 2002, pp. 109–128; Diller + Scofidio, *Expo.02 Yverdon-les-Bains Arteplage: The Cloud*, in A + U: «Architecture and Urbanism», n. 8 (383), August 2002, pp. 28–35; Fred Bernstein, *At the Land of Three Lakes, Swiss Expo.02, floats a potpourri of architectural expressions*, in «Architectural Record», vol. 190 n. 8, August 2002, p. 74, 76; Catherine Slessor, *Blurring reality*, in «The Architectural Review», vol. 212, September 2002, pp. 46–47; Luca Zevi, *Poetica del dubbio / Poetics of uncertainty*, in «L'architettura – Cronache e Storia», vol. 48, October 2002, pp. 658–659; Diller + Scofidio, *Expo.02 - Arteplage*, in «Quaderns», n. 236, January 2003, pp. 118–123.
An extraordinary document is the text D + S 2002, an authentic daily diary on the construction of the *Blur Building*.
To further the field of understanding of the themes involving the shapeless in art and philosophy see: Honoré de Balzac, *Il capolavoro sconosciuto* [1832], Passigli Editore, Florence 1995; Giovanni Papini, *GOG* [1931], Stabilimenti Grafici Vallecchi, Florence 1945, pp. 131–34 *(La nuova scultura)*; Derrida 2003, p. 167.

Summary

The Information Technology Revolution in Architecture is a series reflecting on the effects the virtual dimension is having on architects and architecture in general. Each volume will examine a single topic, highlighting the essential aspects and exploring their relevance for the architects of today.

Other titles in this series

Diller + Scofidio
Il teatro
della dissolvenza
Antonello Marotta
ISBN 88-7864-010-7 *Italiano*
978-1-4466-7679-0 *Inglese*

Gamezone
Playground tra scenari virtuali
e realtà
Alberto Iacovoni
ISBN 88-7864-011-5

Strati Mobili
Video contestuali
nell'arte e nell'architettura
Alexandro Ladaga & Silvia Manteiga
ISBN 88-7864-016-6

Takis Zenetos
Visioni digitali,
architetture costruite
Dimitris Papalexopoulos, Eleni Kalafati
ISBN 88-7864-012-3

Arie italiane
Motivi dell'architettura
italiana recente
Antonello Marotta, Paola Ruotolo
ISBN 88-7864-022-0

Stanze ribelli
Immaginando
lo spazio hacker
Alexander Levi, Amanda Schachter
ISBN 978-88-7864-028-3

Penezic & Rogina
Digitalizzazione
della realtà
Nigel Whiteley
ISBN 978-88-7864-030-6 *Italiano*
978-1-4461-0015-8 *Inglese*

Ipercorpi
Verso una
architettura e-motiva
Kas Oosterhuis
ISBN 978-88-7864-037-5

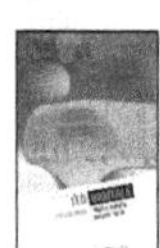

Ito digitale
Nuovi media,
nuovo reale
Patrizia Mello
ISBN 978-88-7864-044-3

SHoP Works
Collaborazioni costruttive
in digitale
Stefano Converso
ISBN 978-88-7864-045-0 *Italiano*
978-1-4478-4748-9 *Inglese*

Cyberstone
Innovazioni digitali
sulla pietra
Christian R. Pongratz, M. Rita Perbellini
ISBN 978-88-7864-051-4

La forma come memoria
Una teoria geometrica
dell'architettura
Michael Leyton
ISBN 978-88-7864-055-9

Van Berkel digitale
Diagrammi, processi, modelli
di UNStudio
Andrea Sollazzo
ISBN 978-88-7864-070-2 *Italiano*
978-1-4478-6706-7 *Inglese*

www.ingramcontent.com/pod-product-compliance
Lightning Source LLC
Chambersburg PA
CBHW060132050426
42448CB00010B/2087